GENERAL INTRODUCTION

TO THE

PHILOSOPHY

AND WRITINGS

OF

PLATO

FROM

THE WORKS OF PLATO:
His Fifty-Five Dialogues and Twelve Epistles, 1804

BY THOMAS TAYLOR

FIRST PUBLISHED, 1804.
RE-PRINTED WITH NEW FORMATTING, 2016.

K **SHETRA**
B **OOKS**
IDEAS EMBODIED.

www.kshetrabooks.com

"General Introduction to the Philosophy and Writings of Plato,"
from *The Works of Plato,*
viz. His Fifty-Five Dialogues, and Twelve Epistles
First Edition, 1804

Re-print from 1st Edition
(with new formatting)

Cover Design adapted from original photograph
"Ancient road to the Academy," by Tomisti.
Source file retrieved March 24, 2016:
https://en.wikipedia.org/wiki/File:Athens_-_Ancient_road_to_Academy_1.jpg
Liscence: Creative Commons Attribution-Share Alike 3.0 Unported.

ISBN: 978-1530752379

Contents

Foreword..V

General Introduction...7

Explanation of Certain Platonic Terms...93

The Life of Plato by Olympiodorus..105

Notes...III

Foreword

The *General Introduction* contained in the present volume is drawn from Thomas Taylor's five-volume set of the complete *Works of Plato*, originally published in 1804. With that great task completed, Taylor became the first to translate the whole of the genuine works of Plato (his 55 dialogues and 12 epistles) into English. That work is a timeless masterpiece not solely because of the quantity of works translated or the sublimity of those works, but due also to Taylor's ability to elucidate the principles of that philosophy as no other has done in the English tongue.

In his introduction Taylor gives us an overview of the fundamental principles of the philosophy and theology of Plato, guiding us on a journey transcending the mundane particulars of our sensory lives upwards to the summit of all things, the principle of principles and fountain of all that is. Through this journey, and with careful thought and consideration, the student may gather enough of an outline to begin assembling his own conception of that system, from which he may later begin his efforts towards a recollection of divine truths.

Following Taylor's overview of Plato's philosophy, he provides an outline of that great philosopher's writings, from their structure and organization, down to Plato's style of writing. Lastly, Taylor introduces us to the full set of his translations, providing the reasoning used in his arrangement of the dialogues along with references to previous translations and commentaries he relied upon in his efforts.

In his five-volume set, Taylor followed this Introduction with a short glossary of terms peculiar to the Platonic philosophy, which we have here reproduced along with several additional terms and definitions drawn from two of Taylor's other publications.

Concluding this volume, and Taylor's introductory material for his translations, is his rendering of the biography of Plato by Olympiodorus. This biography is rather concise in itself, but provides some general sense of the life of the man.

These introductory materials ought to furnish the sincere student with the necessaries to begin an earnest study of philosophy, not as it is so commonly presented in our modern times, stripped of all substance in the name of ever expanding sophistry, but imbibed with the life-essence of that great wisdom that underlies the genuine Grecian system, from Orpheus to Pythagoras, Plato and beyond. To begin this study is to ask the aid of that golden chain of philosophers in the effort of seeking real knowledge of ourselves, such that we may practice and embody the highest virtue.

The present volume is the first in a series of publications reproducing the *Works of Plato*. It is highly recommended that the student follow Taylor's arrangement of the dialogues in their initial study of the philosophy, in order that they may gain the most from such sincere efforts towards wisdom. If the student is desirous of this, the first dialogue in that arrangement is the *First Alcibiades*. In that dialogue, one will encounter the first, and most critical step in the life of a philosopher: that of liberation from the disease of two-fold ignorance. Only once liberated may one truly benefit from further study of Plato's sublime philosophy.

It is further recommended that the sincere student open themselves to a wider study of the Grecian philosophy, theology and mythology as presented throughout the translations and original works of Thomas Taylor. From the *Egyptian Mysteries*, the *Chaldean Oracles*, the *Hymns of Orpheus*, to the *Life of Pythagoras*, and onwards through the works of Plato, Aristotle and the later Platonists (in particular, that of Proclus), Taylor's translations, as well as his introductions and copious notes, shed clear white light on this vast and sublime wisdom tradition. The study of Plato is but one thread in this divine tapestry.

GENERAL INTRODUCTION
TO
THE PHILOSOPHY AND WRITINGS
OF
PLATO

"Philosophy," says Hierocles,[1] "is the purification and perfection of human life. It is the purification, indeed, from material irrationality, and the mortal body; but the perfection, in consequence of being the resumption of our proper felicity, and a re-ascent to the divine likeness. To effect these two is the province of *Virtue* and *Truth;* the former exterminating the immoderation of the passions; and the latter introducing the divine form to those who are naturally adapted to its reception."

Of philosophy thus defined, which may be compared to a luminous pyramid, terminating in Deity, and having for its basis the rational soul of man and its spontaneous unperverted conceptions,—of this philosophy, august, magnificent, and divine, Plato may be justly called the primary leader and hierophant, through whom, like the mystic light in the inmost recesses of some sacred temple, it first shone forth with occult and venerable splendor.[2] It may indeed be truly said of the whole of this philosophy, that it is the greatest good which man can participate: for if it purifies us from the defilements of the passions and assimilates us to Divinity, it confers on us the proper felicity of our nature. Hence it is easy to collect its pre-eminence to all other philosophies; to show that where they oppose it they are erroneous; that so far as they contain any thing scientific they are allied to it; and that at best they are but rivulets derived from this vast ocean of truth.

To evince that the philosophy of Plato possesses this pre-eminence; that its dignity and sublimity are unrivalled; that it is the parent of all that ennobles man; and that it is founded on principles, which neither time can obliterate, nor sophistry subvert, is the principal design of this Introduction.

To effect this design, I shall in the first place present the reader with the outlines of the principal dogmas of Plato's philosophy. The undertaking is indeed no less novel than arduous, since the author of it has to tread in paths which have been untrodden for upwards of a thousand years, and to bring to light truths which for that extended period have been concealed in Greek. Let not the reader, therefore, be surprised at the solitariness of the paths through which I shall attempt to conduct him, or at the novelty of the objects which will present themselves in the journey: for perhaps he may fortunately recollect that he has travelled the same road before, that the scenes were once familiar to him, and that the country through which he is passing is his native land. At least, if his sight should be dim, and his memory oblivious, (for the objects which he will meet with can only be seen by the most piercing eyes,) and his absence from them has been lamentably long, let him implore the power of wisdom,

> From mortal mists to purify his eyes,
> That God and man he may distinctly see.
> Αχλυν δ' αυ τοι απ' οφθαλμων ελον, η πριν επηεν,
> Οφρ' ευ γινωσκης ημεν Θεον, ηδε και ανδρα.
> Iliad. V. v. 127, etc.

Let us also, imploring the assistance of the same illuminating power, begin the solitary journey.

Of all the dogmas of Plato, that concerning the first principle of things as far transcends in sublimity the doctrine of other philosophers of a different sect, on this subject, as this supreme cause of all transcends other causes. For, according to Plato, the highest God, whom in the Republic he calls *the good*, and in the Parmenides *the one*, is not only above soul and intellect, but is even superior to being itself. Hence, since every thing which can in any respect be known, or of which any thing can be asserted, must be connected with the universality of things, but the first cause is above all things, it is very properly said by Plato to be perfectly ineffable. The first hypothesis therefore of his Parmenides, in which all things are denied of this immense principle, concludes as follows:

> "*The one* therefore *is* in no respect. So it seems. Hence it is not in such a manner as *to be* one, for thus it would be *being*, and participate of *essence:* but as it appears, *the one* neither *is one*, nor *is*, if it be proper to believe in reasoning of this kind. It appears so. But can any thing either belong to, or be affirmed of that which is not? How can it? Neither therefore does any *name* belong to it, nor *discourse*, nor any *science*, nor *sense*, nor *opinion*. It does not appear that there can. Hence it can neither be *named*, nor *spoken of*, nor *conceived by opinion*, nor be *known*, nor *perceived* by any being. So it seems."

And here it must be observed that this conclusion respecting the highest principle of things, that he is perfectly ineffable and inconceivable, is the result of a most scientific series of negations, in which not only all sensible and intellectual beings are denied of him, but even natures the most transcendently allied to him, his first and most divine progeny. For that which so eminently distinguishes the philosophy of Plato from others is this, that every part of it is stamped with the character of science. The vulgar indeed proclaim the Deity to be ineffable; but as they have no scientific knowledge that he is so, this is nothing more than a confused and indistinct perception of the most sublime of all truths, like that of a thing seen between sleeping and waking, like Phæacia to Ulysses when sailing to his native land,

> That lay before him indistinct and vast,
> Like a broad shield amid the watr'y waste.[3]

In short, an unscientific perception of the ineffable nature of the Divinity resembles that of a man, who, on surveying the heavens, should assert of the altitude of its highest part, that it surpasses that of the loftiest tree, and is therefore immeasurable. But to see this scientifically, is like a survey of this highest part of the heavens by the astronomer: for he, by knowing the height of the media between us and it, knows also scientifically that it transcends in altitude not only the loftiest tree, but the summits of air and æther, the moon, and even the sun itself.

Let us therefore investigate what is the ascent to the ineffable, and after what manner it is accomplished, according to Plato, from the last of things, following the profound and most inquisitive[4] Damascius as our leader in this arduous investigation. Let our discourse also be common to other principles, and to things proceeding from them to that which is last; and let us, beginning from that which is perfectly effable and known to sense, ascend to the ineffable, and establish in silence, as in a port, the parturitions of truth concerning it. Let us then assume the following axiom, in which as in a secure vehicle we may safely pass from hence thither. I say, therefore, that the unindigent is naturally prior to the indigent. For that which is in want of another is naturally adapted from necessity to be subservient to that of which it is indigent. But if they are mutually in want of each other, each being indigent of the other in a different respect, neither of them will be the principle. For the unindigent is most adapted to that which is truly the principle. And if it is in want of any thing, according to this it will not be the principle. It is however necessary that the principle should be this very thing, the principle alone. The unindigent therefore pertains to this, nor must it by any means be acknowledged that there is any thing prior to it. This, however, would be acknowledged, if it had any connection with the indigent.

Let us then consider body, (that is, a triply extended substance,) endued with quality; for this is the first thing effable by us, and is sensible. Is this then the principle of things? But it is two things, body, and quality which is in body as a subject. Which of these therefore is by nature prior? For both are indigent of their proper parts: and that also which is in a subject is indigent of the subject. Shall we say then that body itself is the principle and the first essence? But this is impossible. For, in the first place, the principle will not receive any thing from that which is posterior to itself. But body, we say, is the recipient of quality. Hence quality, and a subsistence in conjunction with it, are not derived from body, since quality is present with body as something different. And, in the second place, body is every way divisible; its several parts are indigent of each other, and the whole is indigent of all the parts. As it is indigent, therefore, and receives its completion from things which are indigent, it will not be entirely unindigent.

Further still, if it is not one but united, it will require, as Plato says, the connecting one. It is likewise something common and formless, being as it were a certain matter. It requires, therefore, ornament and the possession of form, that it may not be merely body, but a body with a certain particular quality; as, for instance, a fiery or earthly body, and, in short, body adorned and invested with a particular quality. Hence the things which accede to it, finish and adorn it. Is then that which accedes the principle? But this is impossible. For it does not abide in itself, nor does it subsist alone, but is in a subject, of which also it is indigent. If, however, some one should assert that body is not a subject, but one of the elements in each, as, for instance, animal in horse and man, thus also each will be indigent of the other, *viz.* this subject, and that which is in the subject; or rather the common element, animal, and the peculiarities, as the rational and irrational, will be indigent. For elements are always indigent of each other, and that which is composed from elements is indigent of the elements. In short, this sensible nature, and which is so manifest to us, is neither body; for this does not of itself move the senses, nor quality; for this does not possess an interval commensurate with sense. Hence, that which is the object of sight, is neither body nor colour; but coloured body, or colour corporalized, is that which is motive of the sight. And universally that which is sensible, which is body with a particular quality, is motive of sense. From hence, it is evident that the thing which excites the sense is something incorporeal. For if it was body, it would not yet be the object of sense. Body therefore requires that which is incorporeal, and that which is incorporeal, body. For an incorporeal nature is not of itself sensible. It is, however, different from body, because these two possess prerogatives different from each other, and neither of these subsists prior to the other; but being elements of one sensible thing, they are present with each other; the one imparting interval to that which is void of interval, but the other introducing to that which is formless, sensible variety invested with form. In the third place, neither are both these together the principle; since they are not unindigent. For they stand in need of their proper elements, and of that which conducts them to the generation of one form. For body cannot effect this, since it is of itself impotent; nor quality, since it is not able to subsist separate from the body in which it is, or together with which it has its being. The composite therefore either produces itself, which is impossible, for it does not converge to itself, but the whole of it is multifariously dispersed, or it is not produced by itself, and there is some other principle prior to it.

Let it then be supposed to be that which is called nature, being a principle of motion and rest, in that which is moved and at rest, essentially and not according to accident. For this is something more simple, and is fabricative of composite forms. If, however, it is in the things fabricated, and does not subsist separate from, nor prior to them, but stands in need of them for its being, it will not be unindigent; though it possesses something transcendent with respect to them, *viz.* the power of fashioning and fabricating them. For it has its being together with them, and has in them an inseparable subsistence; so that when they are it is, and is not when they are not, and this in consequence of perfectly verging to them, and not being able to sustain that which is appropriate. For the power of increasing, nourishing, and generating similars, and the one prior to these three, *viz.* nature, is not wholly incorporeal, but is nearly a certain quality of body, from which it alone differs, in that it imparts to the composite to be inwardly moved and at rest. For the quality of that which is sensible imparts that which is apparent in matter, and that which falls on sense. But body imparts interval every way extended; and nature, an inwardly proceeding natural energy, whether according to place only, or according to nourishing, increasing, and generating things similar. Nature, however, is inseparable from a subject, and is indigent, so that it will not be in short the principle, since it is indigent of that which is subordinate. For it will not be wonderful, if being a certain principle, it is indigent of the principle above it; but it would be wonderful, if it were indigent of things posterior to itself, and of which it is supposed to be the principle.

By the like arguments we may show that the principle cannot be irrational soul, whether sensitive, or orectic. For if it appears that it has something separate, together with impulsive and gnostic energies, yet at the same time, it is bound in body, and has something inseparable from it; since it is not able to convert itself to itself, but its energy is mingled with its subject. For it is evident that its essence is something of this kind; since if it were liberated, and in itself free, it would also evince a certain independent energy, and would not always be converted to body; but sometimes it would be converted to itself; or though it were always converted to body, yet it would judge and explore itself. The energies, therefore, of the multitude of mankind, though they are conversant with externals, yet at the same time they exhibit that which is separate about them. For they consult how they should engage in them, and observe that deliberation is necessary, in order to effect or be passive to apparent good, or to decline something of the contrary. But the impulses of other irrational animals are uniform and spontaneous, are moved together with the sensible organs, and require the senses alone that they may obtain from sensibles the pleasurable, and avoid the painful. If, therefore, the body communicates in pleasure and pain, and is affected in a certain respect by them, it is evident that the psychical energies (*i.e.* energies belonging to the soul) are exerted, mingled with bodies, and are not purely psychical, but are also corporeal; for perception is of the animated body, or of the soul corporalized, though in such perception the psychical idiom predominates over the corporeal; just as in bodies the corporeal idiom has dominion according to interval and subsistence. As the irrational soul, therefore, has its being in something different from itself, so far it is indigent of the subordinate: but a thing of this kind will not be the principle.

Prior then to this essence, we see a certain form separate from a subject, and converted to itself, such as is the rational nature. Our soul, therefore, presides over its proper energies, and corrects itself. This, however, would not be the case, unless it was converted to itself; and it would not be converted to itself unless it had a separate essence. It is not therefore indigent of the subordinate. Shall we then say that it is the most perfect principle? But it does not at once exert all its energies, but is always indigent of the greater part. The principle, however, wishes to have nothing indigent: but the rational nature is an essence in want of its own energies. Some one, however, may say that it is an eternal essence, and has never-failing essential energies, always concurring with its essence, according to the self-moved, and ever vital, and that it is therefore unindigent, and will be the principle. To this we reply, that the whole soul is one form and one nature, partly unindigent and partly indigent; but the principle is perfectly unindigent. Soul therefore, and which exerts mutable energies, will not be the most proper principle. Hence it is necessary that there should be something prior to this, which is in every respect immutable, according to nature, life, and knowledge, and according to all powers and energies, such as we assert an eternal and immutable essence to be, and such as is much honoured intellect, to which Aristotle having ascended, thought he had discovered the first principle. For what can be wanting to that which perfectly comprehends in itself its own plenitudes (πληρωματα), and of which neither addition nor ablation changes any thing belonging to it? Or is not this also, one and many, whole and parts, containing in itself, things first, middle, and last? The subordinate plenitudes also stand in need of the more excellent, and the more excellent of the subordinate, and the whole of the parts. For the things related are indigent of each other, and what are first of what are last, through the same cause; for it is not of itself that which is first. Besides *the one* here is indigent of *the many*, because it has its subsistence in *the many*. Or it may be said, that this one is collective of the many, and this not by itself, but in conjunction with them. Hence there is much of the indigent in this principle. For since intellect generates in itself its proper plenitudes from which the whole at once receives its completion, it will be itself indigent of itself, not only that which is generated of that which generates, but also that which generates of that which is generated, in order to the whole completion of that which wholly generates itself. Further still, intellect understands and is understood, is intellective of and intelligible to itself, and both these. Hence the intellectual is indigent of the intelligible, as of its proper object of desire; and the intelligible is in want of the intellectual, because it wishes to be the intelligible of it. Both also are indigent of either, since the possession is always accompanied with indigence, in the same manner as the world is always present with matter. Hence a certain indigence is naturally coessentiallized with intellect, so that it cannot be the most proper principle. Shall we, therefore, in the next place, direct our attention to the most simple of beings, which Plato calls *the one being*, εν ον? For as there is no separation there throughout the whole, nor any multitude, or order, or duplicity, or conversion to itself, what indigence will there appear to be in the perfectly united? And especially what indigence will there be of that which is subordinate? Hence the great Permenides ascended to this most safe principle, all that which is most unindigent. Is it not, however, here necessary to attend to the conception of Plato, that the united is not *the one itself*, but that which is passive[5] to it? And this being the case, it is evident that it ranks after *the one;* for it is supposed to be *the united* and not *the one itself.* If also being is composed from the elements *bound* and *infinity*, as appears from the Philebus of Plato, where he calls it that which is mixed, it will be indigent of its elements. Besides, if the conception of *being* is different from that of *being united*, and that which is a whole is both united and being, these will be indigent of each other, and the whole which is called *one being* is indigent of the two. And though *the one* in this is better than *being*, yet this is indigent of being, in order to the subsistence of one being. But if *being* here supervenes *the one*, as it were, form in that which is mixed and united, just as the idiom of man in that which is collectively rational-mortal-animal, thus also *the one* will be indigent of *being.* If, however, to speak more properly, *the one* is two-fold, *this* being the cause of the mixture, and subsisting prior to being, but *that* conferring rectitude on being,—if this be the case, neither will the indigent perfectly desert this nature. After all these, it may be said that *the one* will be perfectly unindigent. For neither is it indigent of that which is posterior to itself for its subsistence, since the truly one is by itself separated from all things; nor is it indigent of that which is inferior or more excellent in itself; for there is nothing in it besides itself; nor is it in want of itself. But it is one, because neither has it any duplicity with respect to itself. For not even the relation of itself to itself must be asserted of the truly one; since it is perfectly simple. This, therefore, is the most unindigent of all things. Hence this is the principle and the cause of all; and this is at once the first of all things. If these qualities, however, are present with it, it will not be *the one.*

Or may we not say that all things subsist in *the one* according to *the one?* And that both these subsist in it, and such other things as we predicate of it, as, for instance, the most simple, the most excellent, the most powerful, the preserver of all things, and the good itself? If these things, however, are thus true of *the one*, it will thus also be indigent of things posterior to itself, according to those very things which we add to it. For the principle is and is said to be the principle of things proceeding from it, and the cause is the cause of things caused, and the first is the first of things arranged posterior to it.[6] Further still, the simple subsists according to a transcendency of other things, the most powerful according to power with relation to the subjects of it; and the good, the desirable, and the preserving, are so called with reference to things benefited, preserved, and desiring. And if it should be said, to be all things according to the pre-assumption of all things in itself, it will indeed be said to be so according to *the one* alone, and will at the same time be the one cause of all things prior to all, and will be this and no other according to *the one.* So far, therefore, as it is *the one* alone, it will be unindigent; but so far as unindigent, it will be the first principle and stable root of all principles. So far, however, as it is the principle and the first cause of all things, and is pre-established as the object of desire to all things, so far it appears to be in a certain respect indigent of the things to which it is related. It has therefore, if it be lawful so to speak, an ultimate vestige of indigence, just as on the contrary matter has an ultimate echo of the unindigent, or a most obscure and debile impression of *the one.* And language indeed appears to be here subverted. For so far as it is *the one*, it is also unindigent, since the principle has appeared to subsist according to the most unindigent and *the one.* At the same time, however, so far as it is *the one*, it is also the principle; and so far as it is *the one* it is unindigent, but so far as the principle, indigent. Hence so far as it is unindigent, it is also indigent, though not according to the same; but with respect to being that which it is, it is unindigent; but as producing and comprehending other things in itself, it is indigent. This, however, is the peculiarity of *the one; so* that it is both unindigent and indigent according to *the one.* Not indeed that it is each of these, in such a manner as we divide it in speaking of it, but it is one alone; and according to this is both other things, and that which is indigent. For how is it possible it should not be indigent also so far as it is *the one?* Just as it is all other things which proceed from it. For the indigent also is something belonging to all things. Something else, therefore, must be investigated which in no respect has any kind of indigence. But of a thing of this kind it cannot with truth be asserted that it is the principle, nor can it even be said of it that it is most unindigent, though this appears to be the most venerable of all assertions.[7] For this signifies transcendency, and an exemption from the indigent. We do not, however, think it proper to call this even *the perfectly exempt;* but that which is in every respect incapable of being apprehended, and about which we must be perfectly silent, will be the most just axiom of our conception in the present investigation; nor yet this as uttering any thing, but as rejoicing in not uttering, and by this venerating that immense unknown. This then is the mode of ascent to that which is called the first, or rather to that which is beyond every thing which can be conceived, or become the subject of hypothesis.

There is also another mode, which does not place the unindigent before the indigent, but considers that which is indigent of a more excellent nature, as subsisting secondary to that which is more excellent. Every where then, that which is in capacity is secondary to that which is in energy. For that it may proceed into energy, and that it may not remain in capacity in vain, it requires that which is in energy. For the more excellent never blossoms from the subordinate nature. Let this then be previously defined by us, according to common unperverted conceptions. Matter therefore has prior to itself material form; because all matter is form in capacity, whether it be the first matter which is perfectly formless, or the second which subsists according to body void of quality, or in other words mere triple extension, to which it is likely those directed their attention who first investigated sensibles, and which at first appeared to be the only things that had a subsistence. For the existence of that which is common in the different elements, persuaded them that there is a certain body void of quality. But since, among bodies of this kind, some possess the governing principle inwardly, and others externally, such as things artificial, it is necessary besides quality to direct our attention to nature, as being something better than qualities, and which is prearranged in the order of cause, as art is of things artificial. Of things, however, which are inwardly governed, some appear to possess being alone, but others to be nourished and increased, and to generate things similar to themselves. There is therefore another certain cause prior to the above-mentioned nature, *viz.* a vegetable power itself. But it is evident that all such things as are ingenerated in body as in a subject, are of themselves incorporeal, though they become corporeal by the participation of that in which they subsist, so that they are said to be and are material in consequence of what they suffer from matter. Qualities therefore, and still more natures, and in a still greater degree the vegetable life, preserve the incorporeal in themselves. Since, however, sense exhibits another more conspicuous life, pertaining to beings which are moved according to impulse and place, this must be established prior to that, as being a more proper principle, and as the supplier of a certain better form, that of a self-moved animal, and which naturally precedes plants rooted in the earth. The animal, however, is not accurately self-moved. For the whole is not such throughout the whole; but a part moves, and a part is moved. This therefore is the apparent self-moved. Hence, prior to this it is necessary there should be that which is truly self-moved, and which according to the whole of itself moves and is moved, that the apparently self-moved may be the image of this. And indeed the soul which moves the body, must be considered as a more proper self-moved essence. This, however, is two-fold, the one rational, the other irrational. For that there is a rational soul is evident: or has not every one a cosensation of himself, more clear or more obscure, when converted to himself in the attentions to and investigations of himself, and in the vital and gnostic animadversions of himself? For the essence which is capable of this, and which can collect universals by reasoning, will very justly be rational. The irrational soul also, though it does not appear to investigate these things, and to reason with itself, yet at the same time it moves bodies from place to place, being itself previously moved from itself; for at different times it exerts a different impulse. Does it therefore move itself from one impulse to another? or is it moved by something else, as, for instance, by the whole rational soul in the universe? But it would be absurd to say that the energies of every irrational soul are not the energies of that soul; but of one more divine; since they are infinite, and mingled with much of the base and imperfect. For this would be just the same as to say that the irrational energies are the energies of the rational soul. I omit to mention the absurdity of supposing that the whole essence is not generative of its proper energies. For if the irrational soul is a certain essence, it will have peculiar energies of its own; not imparted from something else, but proceeding from itself. The irrational soul, therefore, will also move itself at different times to different impulses. But if it moves itself, it will be converted to itself. If, however, this be the case, it will have a separate subsistence, and will not be in a subject. It is therefore rational, if it looks to itself: for in being converted to, it surveys, itself. For when extended to things external, it looks to externals, or rather it looks to coloured body, but does not see itself, because sight itself is neither body nor that which is coloured. Hence it does not revert to itself. Neither therefore is this the case with any other irrational nature. For neither does the phantasy project a type of itself, but of that which is sensible, as for instance of coloured body. Nor does irrational appetite desire itself, but aspires after a certain object of desire, such as honour, or pleasure, or riches. It does not therefore move itself.

But if some one, on seeing that brutes exert rational energies, should apprehend that these also participate of the first self-moved, and on this account possess a soul converted to itself, it may perhaps be granted to him that these also are rational natures, except that they are not so essentially, but according to participation, and this most obscure, just as the rational soul may be said to be intellectual according to participation, as always projecting common conceptions without distortion. It must however be observed, that the extremes are, that which is capable of being perfectly separated, such as the rational form, and that which is perfectly inseparable, such as corporeal quality, and that in the middle of these nature subsists, which verges to the inseparable, having a small representation of the separable, and the irrational soul, which verges to the separable; for it appears in a certain respect to subsist by itself separate from a subject; so that it becomes doubtful whether it is self-motive, or alter-motive. For it contains an abundant vestige of self-motion, but not that which is true, and converted to itself, and on this account perfectly separated from a subject. And the vegetable soul has in a certain respect a middle subsistence. On this account, to some of the ancients, it appeared to be a certain soul, but to others, nature.

Again, therefore, that we may return to the proposed object of investigation, how can a self-motive nature of this kind, which is mingled with the alter-motive, be the first principle of things? For it neither subsists from itself, nor does it in reality perfect itself; but it requires a certain other nature both for its subsistence and perfection: and prior to it is that which is truly self-moved. Is therefore that which is properly self-moved the principle, and is it indigent of no form more excellent than itself? Or is not that which moves always naturally prior to that which is moved; and in short does not every form which is pure from its contrary subsist by itself prior to that which is mingled with it? And is not the pure the cause of the comingled? For that which is coessentiallized with another, has also an energy mingled with that other. So that a self-moved nature will indeed make itself; but thus subsisting it will be at the same time moving and moved, but will not be made a moving nature only. For neither is it this alone. Every form however is always alone according to its first subsistence; so that there will be that which moves only without being moved. And indeed it would be absurd that there should be that which is moved only, such as body, but that prior both to that which is self-moved and that which is moved only, there should not be that which moves only. For it is evident that there must be, since this will be a more excellent nature, and that which is is self-moved, so far as it moves itself, is more excellent than so far as it is moved. It is necessary therefore that the essence which moves unmoved should be first, as that which is moved not being motive, is the third, in the middle of which is the self-moved, which we say requires that which moves in order to its becoming motive. In short, if it is moved, it will not abide, so far as it is moved; and if it moves, it is necessary it should *remain* moving so far as it moves. Whence then does it derive the power of *abiding?* For from itself it derives the power either of being moved only, or of at the same time abiding and being moved wholly according to the same. Whence then does it simply obtain the power of abiding? Certainly from that which simply abides. But this is an immovable cause. We must therefore admit that the immovable is prior to the self-moved. Let us consider then if the immovable is the most proper principle? But how is this possible? For the immovable contains as numerous a multitude immovably, as the self-moved self-moveably. Besides an immovable separation must necessarily subsist prior to a self-moveable separation. The unmoved therefore is at the same time one and many, and is at the same time united and separated, and a nature of this kind is denominated intellect. But it is evident that the united in this is naturally prior to and more honourable than the separated. For separation is always indigent of union; but not, on the contrary, union of separation. Intellect, however, has not the united pure from its opposite. For intellectual form is coessentiallized with the separated through the whole of itself. Hence that which is in a certain respect united requires that which is simply united; and that which subsists with another is indigent of that which subsists by itself; and that which subsists according to participation, of that which subsists according to essence. For intellect being self-subsistent produces itself as united, and at the same time separated. Hence it subsists according to both these. It is produced therefore from that which is simply united and alone united. Prior therefore to that which is formal is the uncircumscribed, and undistributed into forms. And this is that which we call the united, and which the wise men of antiquity denominated *being*, possessing in one contraction multitude, subsisting prior to the many.

Having therefore arrived thus far, let us here rest for a while, and consider with ourselves, whether being is the investigated principle of all things. For what will there be which does not participate of being? May we not say, that this, if it is the united, will be secondary to *the one*, and that by participating of *the one* it becomes the united? But in short if we conceive *the one* to be something different from being, if being is prior to *the one*, it will not participate of *the one*. It will therefore be many only, and these will be infinitely infinites. But if *the one* is with *being*, and *being* with *the one*, and they are either coordinate or divided from each other, there will be two principles, and the above-mentioned absurdity will happen. Or they will mutually participate of each other, and there will be two elements. Or they are parts of something else consisting from both. And if this be the case, what will that be which leads them to union with each other? For if *the one* unites being to itself (for this may be said), *the one* also will energize prior to being, that it may call forth and convert being to itself. *The one*, therefore, will subsist from itself self-perfect prior to being. Further still, the more simple is always prior to the more composite. If therefore they are similarly simple, there will either be two principles, or one from the two, and this will be a composite. Hence the simple and perfectly incomposite is prior to this, which must be either one, or not one; and if not one, it must either be many, or nothing. But with respect to nothing, if it signifies that which is perfectly void, it will signify something vain. But if it signifies the arcane, this will not even be that which is simple. In short, we cannot conceive any principle more simple than *the one*. *The one* therefore is in every respect prior to *being*. Hence this is the principle of all things, and Plato recurring to this, did not require any other principle in his reasonings. For the arcane in which this our ascent terminates is not the principle of reasoning, nor of knowledge, nor of animals, nor of beings, nor of unities, but simply of all things, being arranged above every conception and suspicion that we can frame. Hence Plato indicates nothing concerning it, but makes his negations of all other things except *the one*, from *the one*. For that *the one* is he denies in the last place, but he does not make a negation of *the one*. He also, besides this, even denies this negation, but not *the one*. He denies, too, name and conception, and all knowledge, and what can be said more, whole itself and every being. But let there be the united and the unical, and, if you will, the two principles *bound* and *the infinite*. Plato, however, never in any respect makes a negation of *the one* which is beyond all these. Hence in the Sophista he considers it as *the one* prior to being, and in the Republic as *the good* beyond every essence; but at the same time *the one* alone is left. Whether however is it known and effable, or unknown and ineffable? Or is it in a certain respect these, and in a certain respect not? For by a negation of this it may be said the ineffable is affirmed. And again, by the simplicity of knowledge it will be known or suspected, but by composition perfectly unknown. Hence neither will it be apprehended by negation. And in short, so far as it is admitted to be one, so far it will be coarranged with other things which are the subject of position. For it is the summit of things which subsist according to position. At the same time there is much in it of the ineffable and unknown, the uncoordinated, and that which is deprived of position, but these are accompanied with a representation of the contraries: and the former are more excellent than the latter. But every where things pure subsist prior to their contraries, and such as are unmingled to the comingled. For either things more excellent subsist in *the one* essentially, and in a certain respect the contraries of these also will be there at the same time; or they subsist according to participation, and are derived from that which is first a thing of this kind. Prior to *the one*, therefore, is that which is simply and perfectly ineffable, without position, uncoordinated, and incapable of being apprehended, to which also the ascent of the present discourse hastens through the clearest indications, omitting none of those natures between the first and the last of things.

Such then is the ascent to the highest God according to the theology of Plato, venerably preserving his ineffable exemption from all things, and his transcendency, which cannot be circumscribed by any gnostic energy; and at the same time unfolding the paths which lead upwards to him, and enkindling that luminous summit of the soul, by which she is conjoined with the incomprehensible one.

From this truly ineffable principle, exempt from all essence, power, and energy, a multitude of divine natures, according to Plato, immediately proceeds. That this must necessarily be the case will be admitted by the reader who understands what has been already discussed, and is fully demonstrated by Plato in the Parmenides, as will be evident to the intelligent from the notes on that Dialogue. In addition therefore to what I have said on this subject, I shall further observe at present, that this doctrine, which is founded in the sublimest and most scientific conceptions of the human mind, may be clearly shown to be a legitimate dogma of Plato from what is asserted by him in the sixth book of his Republic. For he there affirms, in the most clear and unequivocal terms, that *the good*, or the ineffable principle of things, is superessential, and shows by the analogy of the sun to *the good*, that what *light* and *sight* are in the visible, that *truth* and *intelligence* are in the intelligible world. As light therefore immediately proceeds from the sun, and wholly subsists according to a solar idiom or property, so *truth*, or the immediate progeny of *the good*, must subsist according to a superessential idiom. And as *the good*, according to Plato, is the same with *the one*, as is evident from the Parmenides, the immediate progeny of *the one* will be the same as that of *the good*. But the immediate offspring of *the one* cannot be any thing else than unities. And hence we necessarily infer that, according to Plato, the immediate offspring of the ineffable principle of things are superessential unities. They differ however from their immense principle in this, that he is superessential and ineffable, without any addition; but this divine multitude is participated by the several orders of being, which are suspended from and produced by it. Hence, in consequence of being connected with *multitude* through this participation, they are necessarily subordinate to *the one*.

No less admirably, therefore, than Platonically, does Simplicius, in his Commentary on Epictetus,[8] observe on this subject as follows:

"The fountain and principle of all things is *the good:* for that which all things desire, and to which all things are extended, is the principle and end of all things. *The good* also produces from itself all things, first, middle, and last. But it produces such as are first and proximate to itself, similar to itself; one goodness, many goodnesses, one simplicity and unity which transcends all others, many unities, and one principle many principles. For *the one*, the principle, *the good*, and deity, are the same: for deity is the first and the cause of all things. But it is necessary that the first should also be most simple; since whatever is a composite and has multitude is posterior to *the one*. And multitude and things which are not good desire *the good* as being above them: and in short, that which is not itself the principle is from the principle.

"But it is also necessary that the principle of all things should possess the highest, and all, power. For the amplitude of power consists in producing all things from itself, and in giving subsistence to similars prior to things which are dissimilar. Hence the one principle produces many principles, many simplicities, and many goodnesses, proximately from itself. For since all things differ from each other, and are multiplied with their proper differences, each of these multitudes is suspended from its one proper principle. Thus, for instance, all beautiful things, whatever and wherever they may be, whether in souls or in bodies, are suspended from one fountain of beauty. Thus too, whatever possesses symmetry, and whatever is true, and all principles, are in a certain respect connate with the first principle, so far as they are principles and fountains and goodnesses, with an appropriate subjection and analogy. For what the one principle is to all beings, that each of the other principles is to the multitude comprehended under the idiom of its principle. For it is impossible, since each multitude is characterized by a certain difference, that it should not be extended to its proper principle, which illuminates one and the same form to all the individuals of that multitude. For *the one* is the leader of every multitude; and every peculiarity or idiom in the many, is derived to the many from *the one*.

"All partial principles therefore are established in that principle which ranks as a whole, and are comprehended in it, not with interval and multitude, but as parts in the whole, as multitude in *the one*, and number in the monad. For this first principle is all things prior to all: and many principles are multiplied about the one principle, and in the one goodness, many goodnesses are established. This too is not a certain principle like each of the rest: for of these, one is the principle of beauty, another of symmetry, another of truth, and another of something else, but it is simply *principle*. Nor is it simply the principle of beings, but it is the principle of principles. For it is necessary that the idiom of principle, after the same manner as other things, should not begin from multitude, but should be collected into one monad as a summit, and which is the principle of principles.

"Such things therefore as are first produced by the first good, in consequence of being connascent with it, do not recede from essential goodness, since they are immovable and unchanged, and are eternally established in the same blessedness. They are likewise not indigent of the good, because they are goodnesses themselves. All other natures however, being produced by the one good, and many goodnesses, since they fall off from essential goodness, and are not immovably established in the hyparxis of divine goodness, on this account they possess the good according to participation."

From this sublime theory the meaning of that ancient Egyptian dogma, that God is all things, is at once apparent. For the first principle,[9] as Simplicius in the above passage justly observes, is *all things prior to all*; *i.e.* he comprehends all things causally, this being the most transcendent mode of comprehension. As all things therefore, considered as subsisting causally in deity, are *transcendently more excellent* than they are when considered as effects proceeding from him, hence that mighty and all-comprehending whole, the first principle, is said to be all things *prior* to all; priority here denoting exempt transcendency. As the monad and the centre of a circle are images from their simplicity of this greatest of principles, so likewise do they perspicuously shadow forth to us its causal comprehension of all things. For all number may be considered as subsisting occultly in the monad, and the circle in the centre; this occult being the same in each with causal subsistence.

That this conception of causal subsistence is not an hypothesis devised by the latter Platonists, but a genuine dogma of Plato, is evident from what he says in the Philebus; for in that Dialogue he expressly asserts, that in Jupiter a royal intellect and a royal soul subsist *according to cause*. Pherecydes Syrus too, in his Hymn to Jupiter, as cited by Kercher (in Oedip. Egyptiac.), has the following lines:

Ο Θεος εστι κυκλος, τετραγωνος ηδη τριγωνος,
Κεινος δε γραμμη, κεντρον, και παντα προ παντων.

i.e. Jove is a circle, triangle and square,
Centre and line, and *all things before all.*

From which testimonies the antiquity of this sublime doctrine is sufficiently apparent.

And here it is necessary to observe that nearly all philosophers prior to Iamblichus (as we are informed by Damascius[10]) asserted indeed that there is one *superessential* God, but that the other gods had an *essential* subsistence, and were deified by illuminations from *the one*. They likewise said that there is a multitude of superessential unities, who are not self-perfect subsistences, but illuminated unions with deity, imparted to essences by the highest God. That this hypothesis, however, is not conformable to the doctrine of Plato is evident from his Parmenides, in which he shows that *the one* does not subsist in itself.[11] For as we have observed from Proclus, in the notes on that Dialogue, every thing which is the cause of itself and is self-subsistent is said to be in itself. Hence as producing power always comprehends according to cause that which it produces, it is necessary that whatever produces itself should comprehend itself so far as it is a cause, and should be comprehended by itself so far as it is caused; and that it should be at once both cause and the thing caused, that which comprehends, and that which is comprehended. If therefore a subsistence in another signifies, according to Plato, the being produced by another more excellent cause,[12] a subsistence in itself must signify that which is self-begotten, and produced by itself. If *the one* therefore is not self-subsistent as even transcending this mode of subsistence, and if it be necessary that there should be something self-subsistent, it follows that this must be the characteristic property of that which immediately proceeds from the ineffable. But that there must be something self-subsistent is evident, since unless this is admitted there will not be a true sufficiency in any thing.

Besides, as Damascius well observes, if that which is subordinate by nature is self-perfect, such as the human soul, much more will this be the case with a divine soul. But if with soul, this also will be true of intellect. And if it be true of intellect, it will also be true of life: if of life, of being likewise; and if of being, of the unities above being. For the self-perfect, the self-sufficient, and that which is established in itself, will much more subsist in superior than in subordinate natures. If therefore these are in the latter, they will also be in the former, I mean the subsistence of a thing by itself, and essentialized in itself; and such are essence and life, intellect, soul, and body. For body, though it does not subsist from, yet subsists by itself; and through this belongs to the genus of substance, and is contradistinguished from accident, which cannot exist independent of a subject.

Self-subsistent superessential natures therefore are the immediate progeny of *the one*, if it be lawful thus to denominate things, which ought rather to be called ineffable unfoldings into light from the ineffable; for progeny implies a producing cause, and *the one* must be conceived as something more excellent than this. From this divine self-perfect and self-producing multitude, a series of self-perfect natures, *viz.* of beings, lives, intellects, and souls proceeds, according to Plato, in the last link of which luminous series he also classes the human soul; proximately suspended from the dæmoniacal order: for this order, as he clearly asserts in the Banquet,[13] "stands in the middle rank between the divine and human, fills up the vacant space, and links together all intelligent nature." And here to the reader, who has not penetrated the depths of Plato's philosophy, it will doubtless appear paradoxical in the extreme, that any being should be said to produce itself, and yet at the same time proceed from a superior cause. The solution of this difficulty is as follows:

Essential production, or that energy through which any nature produces something else by its very being, is the most perfect mode of production, because vestiges of it are seen in the last of things; thus fire imparts heat by its very essence, and snow coldness. And in short, this is a producing of that kind, in which the effect is that secondarily which the cause is primarily. As this mode of production therefore, from its being the most perfect of all others, originates from the highest natures, it will consequently first belong to those self-subsistent powers, who immediately proceed from the ineffable, and will from them be derived to all the following orders of beings. But this energy, as being characterized by the essential, will necessarily be different in different producing causes. Hence, from that which subsists at the summit of self-subsistent natures, a series of self-subsisting beings will indeed proceed, but then this series will be secondarily that which its cause is primarily, and the energy by which it produces itself will be secondary to that by which it is produced by its cause. Thus, for instance, the rational soul both produces itself (in consequence of being a self-motive nature), and is produced by intellect; but it is produced by intellect *immutably*, and by itself *transitively;* for all its energies subsist in time, and are accompanied with motion. So far therefore as soul contains intellect by participation, so far it is produced by intellect, but so far as it is self-motive it is produced by itself. In short, with respect to every thing self-subsistent, the summit of its nature is produced by a superior cause, but the evolution of that summit is its own spontaneous energy; and through this it becomes self-subsistent and self-perfect.

That the rational soul, indeed, so far as it is rational, produces itself, may be clearly demonstrated as follows:

That which is able to impart any thing superior and more excellent in any genus of things, can easily impart that which is subordinate and less excellent in the same genus; but *well being* confessedly ranks higher and is more excellent than *mere being*. The rational soul imparts *well being* to itself, when it cultivates and perfects itself, and recalls and withdraws itself from the contagion of the body. It will therefore also impart *being* to itself. And this with great propriety; for all divine natures, and such things as possess the ability of imparting any thing primarily to others, necessarily begin this energy from themselves. Of this mighty truth the sun himself is an illustrious example; for he illuminates all things with his light, and is himself light, and the fountain and origin of all splendour. Hence, since the soul imparts life and motion to other things, on which account Aristotle calls an animal αυτοκινητον, *self-moved*, it will much more, and by a much greater priority, impart life and motion to itself.

From this magnificent, sublime, and most scientific doctrine of Plato, respecting the arcane principle of things and his immediate progeny, it follows, that this ineffable cause is not the immediate maker of the universe, and this, as I have observed in the Introduction to the Timæus, not through any defect, but on the contrary through transcendency of power. All things indeed are ineffably unfolded from him *at once*, into light; but divine media are necessary to the fabrication of the world. For if the universe was immediately produced from the ineffable, it would, agreeably to what we have above observed, be ineffable also in a secondary degree. But as this is by no means the case, it principally derives its immediate subsistence from a deity of a fabricative characteristic, whom Plato calls Jupiter, conformably to the theology of Orpheus. The intelligent reader will readily admit that this dogma is so far from being derogatory to the dignity of the Supreme, that on the contrary it exalts that dignity, and preserves in a becoming manner the exempt transcendency of the ineffable. If therefore we presume to celebrate him, for, as we have already observed, it is more becoming to establish in silence those parturitions of the soul which dare anxiously to explore him, we should celebrate him as the principle of principles, and the fountain of deity, or, in the reverential language of the Egyptians, as a darkness thrice unknown. Highly laudable indeed, and worthy the imitation of all posterity, is the veneration which the great ancients paid to this immense principle. This I have already noticed in the Introduction to the Parmenides; and I shall only observe at present in addition, that in consequence of this profound and most pious reverence of the first God, they did not even venture to give a name to the summit of that highest order of divinities which is denominated intelligible. Hence, says Proclus, in his MSS. Scholia on the Cratylus:

> "Not every genus of the gods has an appellation: for with respect to the first Deity, who is beyond all things, Parmenides teaches us that he is ineffable; and the first genera of the intelligible gods, who are united to *the one*, and are called occult, have much of the unknown and ineffable. For that which is perfectly effable cannot be conjoined with the perfectly ineffable; but it is necessary that the progression of intelligibles should terminate in this order, in which the first effable subsists, and that which is called by proper names. For there the first intelligible forms, and the intellectual nature of intelligibles, are unfolded into light. But the natures prior to this being silent and occult, are only known by intelligence. Hence the whole of the telestic science energizing theurgically ascends as far as to this order. Orpheus also says, that this is first called by a name by the other gods; for the light proceeding from it is known to and denominated by the intellectual gods."

With no less magnificence therefore than piety, does Proclus thus speak concerning the ineffable principle of things:

> "Let us now if ever remove from ourselves multiform knowledge, exterminate all the variety of life, and in perfect quiet approach near to the cause of all things. For this purpose, let not only opinion and phantasy be at rest, nor the passions alone which impede our anagogic impulse to *the first* be at peace; but let the air, and the universe itself, be still. And let all things extend us with a tranquil power to communion with the ineffable. Let us also standing there, having transcended the intelligible (if we contain any thing of this kind), and with nearly closed eyes

adoring as it were the rising sun, since it is not lawful for any being whatever intently to behold him,—let us survey the sun whence the light of the intelligible gods proceeds, emerging, as the poets say, from the bosom of the ocean; and again from this divine tranquillity descending into intellect, and from intellect employing the reasonings of the soul, let us relate to ourselves what the natures are, from which in this progression we shall consider the first God as exempt. And let us as it were celebrate him, *not as establishing the earth and the heavens*, nor as giving subsistence to souls, and the generations of all animals; for he produced these indeed, *but among the last of things*. But prior to these, let us celebrate him as unfolding into light the whole intelligible and intellectual genus of gods, together with all the supermundane and mundane divinities,—as the God of all gods, the Unity of all unities, and beyond the first adyta,—as more ineffable than all silence, and more unknown that all essence,—as holy among the holies, and concealed in the intelligible gods."[14]

Such is the piety, such the sublimity and magnificence of conception, with which the Platonic philosophers speak of that which is in reality in every respect ineffable, when they presume to speak about it, extending the ineffable parturitions of the soul to the ineffable co-sensation of *the incomprehensible one.*

From this sublime veneration of this most awful nature, which, as is noticed in the extracts from Damascius, induced the most ancient theologists, philosophers, and poets, to be entirely silent concerning it, arose the great reverence which the ancients paid to the divinities even of a mundane characteristic, or from whom bodies are suspended, considering them also as partaking of the nature of the ineffable, and as so many links of the truly golden chain of deity. Hence we find in the Odyssey,[15] when Ulysses and Telemachus are removing the arms from the walls of the palace of Ithaca, and Minerva going before them with her golden lamp, fills all the place with a divine light,

————παροιθε δε παλλας Αθηνη.
Χρυσεου λυχνον εχουσα, φαος περικαλλες εποιει.

Telemachus having observed that certainly some one of the celestial gods was present,

Η μαλα τις θεος ενδον, οι ουρανον ευρυν εχουσι.

Ulysses says in reply, "Be *silent*, restrain your intellect (*i.e.* even cease to energize intellectually), and speak not."

Σιγα, και κατα σον νοον ισχανε, μηδ' ερεεινη.

Lastly, from all that has been said, it must, I think, be immediately obvious to every one whose mental eye is not entirely blinded, that there can be no such thing as a trinity in the theology of Plato, in any respect analogous to the Christian Trinity. For the highest God, according to Plato, as we have largely shown from irresistible evidence, is so far from being a part of a consubsistent triad, that he is not to be connumerated with any thing; but is so perfectly exempt from all multitude, that he is even beyond being; and he so ineffably transcends all relation and habitude, that language is in reality subverted about him, and knowledge refunded into ignorance. What that trinity however is in the theology of Plato, which doubtless gave birth to the Christian, will be evident to the intelligent from the notes on the Parmenides, and the extracts from Damascius.[16] And thus much for the doctrine of Plato concerning the principle of things, and his immediate offspring, the great importance of which will, I doubt not, be a sufficient apology for the length of this discussion.

In the next place, following Proclus and Olympiodorus as our guides, let us consider the mode according to which Plato teaches us mystic conceptions of divine natures: for he appears not to have pursued every where the same mode of doctrine about these; but sometimes according to a divinely inspired energy, and at other times dialectically he evolves the truth concerning them. And sometimes he symbolically announces their ineffable idioms, but at other times he recurs to them from images, and discovers in them the primary causes of wholes. For in the Phædrus being evidently inspired, and having exchanged human intelligence for a better possession, divine mania, he unfolds many arcane dogmas concerning the *intellectual*, *liberated*, and *mundane* gods. But in the Sophista dialectically contending about being, and the subsistence of *the one* above beings, and doubting against philosophers more ancient than himself, he shows how all beings are suspended from their cause and the first being, but that being itself participates of that unity which is exempt from all things, that it is a passive[17] one, but not *the one itself*, being subject to and united to *the one*, but not being that which is primarily one. In a similar manner too, in the *Parmenides*, he unfolds dialectically the progressions of being from *the one*, through the first hypothesis of that dialogue, and this, as he there asserts, according to the most perfect division of this method. And again in the Gorgias, he relates the fable concerning the three fabricators, and their demiurgic allotment. But in the Banquet he speaks concerning the union of love; and in the Protagoras, about the distribution of mortal animals from the gods; in a symbolical manner concealing the truth concerning divine natures, and as far as to mere indication unfolding his mind to the most genuine of his readers.

Again, if it be necessary to mention the doctrine delivered through the mathematical disciplines, and the discussion of divine concerns from ethical or physical discourses, of which many may be contemplated in the Timæus, many in the dialogue called Politicus, and many may be seen scattered in other dialogues;—here likewise, to those who are desirous of knowing divine concerns through images, the method will be apparent. Thus, for instance, the Politicus shadows forth the fabrication in the heavens. But the figures of the five elements, delivered in geometrical proportions in the Timæus, represent in images the idioms of the gods who preside over the parts of the universe. And the divisions of the essence of the soul in that dialogue shadow forth the total orders of the gods. To this we may also add, that Plato composes polities, assimilating them to divine natures, and adorning them from the whole world and the powers which it contains. All these, therefore, through the similitude of mortal to divine concerns, exhibit to us in images the progressions, orders, and fabrications of the latter. And such are the modes of theologic doctrine employed by Plato.

"But those," says Proclus,[18] "who treat of divine concerns in an indicative manner, either speak symbolically and fabulously, or through images. And of those who openly announce their conceptions, some frame their discourses according to science, but others according to inspiration from the gods. And he who desires to signify divine concerns through symbols is Orphic, and, in short, accords with those who write fables respecting the gods. But he who does this through images is Pythagoric. For the mathematical disciplines were invented by the Pythagoreans, in order to a reminiscence of divine concerns, to which, through these as images, they endeavour to ascend. For they refer both numbers and figures to the gods, according to the testimony of their historians. But the entheastic character, or he who is divinely inspired, unfolding the truth itself concerning the gods essentially, perspicuously ranks among the highest initiators. For these do not think proper to unfold the divine orders, or their idioms, to their familiars through veils, but announce their powers and their numbers, in consequence of being moved by the gods themselves. But the tradition of divine concerns according to science, is the illustrious prerogative of the Platonic philosophy. For Plato alone, as it appears to me of all those who are known to us, has attempted methodically to divide and reduce into order the regular progression of the divine genera, their mutual difference, the common idioms of the total orders, and the distributed idioms in each."

Again, since Plato employs fables, let us in the first place consider whence the ancients were induced to devise fables, and in the second place, what the difference is between the fables of philosophers and those of poets. In answer to the first question then, it is necessary to know, that the ancients employed fables, looking to two things, *viz.* nature, and our soul. They employed them by looking to nature, and the fabrication of things, as follows. Things unapparent are believed from things apparent, and incorporeal natures from bodies. For seeing the orderly arrangement of bodies, we understand that a certain incorporeal power presides over them; as with respect to the celestial bodies, they have a certain presiding motive power. As we therefore see that our body is moved, but is no longer so after death, we conceive that it was a certain incorporeal power which moved it. Hence, perceiving that we believe things incorporeal and unapparent from things apparent and corporeal, fables came to be adopted, that we might come from things apparent to certain unapparent natures; as, for instance, that on hearing the adulteries, bonds, and lacerations of the gods, castrations of heaven, and the like, we may not rest satisfied with the apparent meaning of such like particulars, but may proceed to the unapparent, and investigate the true signification. After this manner, therefore, looking to the nature of things, were fables employed.

But from looking to our souls, they originated as follows: While we are children we live according to the phantasy; but the phantastic part is conversant with figures, and types, and things of this kind. That the phantastic part in us therefore may be preserved, we employ fables, in consequence of this part rejoicing in fables. It may also be said, that a fable is nothing else than a false discourse shadowing forth the truth: for a fable is the image of truth. But the soul is the image of the natures prior to herself: and hence the soul very properly rejoices in fables, as an image in an image. As we are therefore from our childhood nourished in fables, it is necessary that they should be introduced. And thus much for the first problem, concerning the origin of fables.

In the next place let us consider what the difference is between the fables of philosophers[19] and poets. Each therefore has something in which it abounds more than, and something in which it is deficient from, the other. Thus, for instance, the poetic fable abounds in this, that we must not rest satisfied with the apparent meaning, but pass on to the occult truth. For who, endued with intellect, would believe that Jupiter was desirous of having connection with Juno, and on the ground, without waiting to go into the bed-chamber. So that the poetic fable abounds, in consequence of asserting such things as do not suffer us to stop at the apparent, but lead us to explore the occult truth. But it is defective in this, that it deceives those of a juvenile age. Plato therefore neglects fable of this kind, and banishes Homer from his Republic; because youth, on hearing such fables, will not be able to distinguish what is allegorical from what is not.

Philosophical fables, on the contrary, do not injure those that go no further than the apparent meaning. Thus, for instance, they assert that there are punishments and rivers under the earth: and if we adhere to the literal meaning of these we shall not be injured. But they are deficient in this, that as their apparent signification does not injure, we often content ourselves with this, and do not explore the latent truth. We may also say that philosophic fables look to the energies of the soul. For if we were entirely intellect alone, and had no connection with phantasy, we should not require fables, in consequence of always associating with intellectual natures. If, again, we were entirely irrational, and lived according to the phantasy, and had no other energy than this, it would be requisite that the whole of our life should be fabulous. Since, however, we possess intellect, opinion, and phantasy, demonstrations are given with a view to intellect: and hence Plato says, that if you are willing to energize according to intellect, you will have demonstrations bound with adamantine chains; if according to opinion, you will have the testimony of renowned persons; and if according to the phantasy, you have fables by which it is excited; so that from all these you will derive advantage.

Plato therefore rejects the more tragical mode of mythologizing of the ancient poets, who thought proper to establish an arcane theology respecting the gods, and on this account devised wanderings, castrations, battles, and lacerations of the gods, and many other such symbols of the truth about divine natures which this theology conceals;—this mode he rejects, and asserts that it is in every respect most foreign from erudition. But he considers those mythological discourses about the gods, as more persuasive and more adapted to truth, which assert that a divine nature is the cause of all good, but of no evil, and that it is void of all mutation, comprehending in itself the fountain of truth but never becoming the cause of any deception to others. For such types of theology Socrates delivers in the Republic.

All the fables therefore of Plato, guarding the truth in concealment, have not even their externally-apparent apparatus discordant with our undisciplined and unperverted anticipations of divinity. But they bring with them an image of the mundane composition, in which both the apparent beauty is worthy of divinity, and a beauty more divine than this is established in the unapparent lives and powers of its causes.

In the next place, that the reader may see whence, and from what dialogues principally the theological dogmas of Plato may be collected, I shall present him with the following translation of what Proclus[20] has admirably written on this subject.

"The truth," says he, "concerning the gods pervades, as I may say, through all the Platonic dialogues, and in all of them conceptions of the first philosophy, venerable, clear, and supernatural, are disseminated, in some more obscurely, but in others more conspicuously; conceptions which excite those that are in any respect able to partake of them, to the immaterial and separate essence of the gods. And as in each part of the universe and in nature itself, the demiurgus of all which the world contains established resemblances of the unknown essence of the gods, that all things might be converted to a divine nature, through their alliance with it, in like manner I am of opinion, that the divine intellect of Plato weaves conceptions about the gods in all his writings, and leaves nothing deprived of the mention of divinity, that from the whole of them, a reminiscence of wholes may be obtained, and imparted to the genuine lovers of divine concerns.

"But if it be requisite to lay before the reader those dialogues out of many, which principally unfold to us the mystic discipline about the gods, I should not err in ranking among this number, the Phædo and the Phædrus, the Banquet, and the Philebus, and together with these, the Sophista and Politicus, the Cratylus and the Timæus. For all these are full through the whole of themselves, as I may say, of the divine science of Plato. But I should place in the second rank after these, the fable in the Gorgias, and that in the Protagoras; likewise the assertions about the providence of the gods in the Laws and, such things as are delivered about the Fates, or the mother of the Fates, or the circulations of the universe in the tenth book of the Republic. Again, you may, if you please, place in the third rank those Epistles, through which we may be able to arrive at the science about divine natures. For in these, mention is made of the three kings; and very many other divine dogmas worthy of the Platonic theory are delivered. It is necessary therefore, looking to these, to explore in these each order of the gods.

"Thus from the Philebus, we may receive the science respecting the one good, and the two first principles of things (bound and infinity) together with the triad which is unfolded into light from these. For you will find all these distinctly delivered to us by

Plato in that dialogue. But from the Timæus, you may obtain the theory about intelligibles, a divine narration about the demiurgic monad, and the most full truth about the mundane gods. From the Phædrus you may learn all the intelligible and intellectual genera, and the liberated orders of gods, which are proximately established above the celestial circulations. From the Politicus, you may obtain the theory of the fabrication in the heavens, of the periods of the universe, and of the intellectual causes of those periods. But from the Sophista you may learn the whole sublunary generation, and the idiom of the gods who are allotted the sublunary region, and preside over its generations and corruptions. And with respect to each of the gods, we may obtain many sacred conceptions from the Banquet, many from the Cratylus, and many from the Phædo. For in each of these dialogues, more or less mention is made of divine names, from which it is easy for those who are exercised in divine concerns to discover by a reasoning process the idioms of each.

"It is necessary, however, to evince, that each of the dogmas accords with Platonic principles, and the mystic traditions of theologists. For all the Grecian theology is the progeny of the mystic doctrine of Orpheus; Pythagoras first of all learning from Aglaophemus the orgies of the gods, but Plato in the second place receiving an all-perfect science of the divinities from the Pythagoric and Orphic writings. For in the Philebus, referring the theory about the two forms of principles (bound and infinity) to the Pythagoreans, he calls them men dwelling with the gods, and truly blessed. Philolaus, therefore, the Pythagorean, has left us in writing many admirable conceptions about these principles, celebrating their common progression into beings, and their separate fabrication. Again, in the Timæus, endeavouring to teach us about the sublunary gods and their order, Plato flies to theologists, calls them the sons of the gods, and makes them the fathers of the truth about those divinities. And lastly, he delivers the orders of the sublunary gods proceeding from wholes, according to the progression delivered by them of the intellectual kings. Further still, in the Cratylus he follows the traditions of theologists respecting the order of the divine processions. But in the Gorgias he adopts the Homeric dogma, respecting the triadic hypostasis of the demiurgi. And in short, he every where discourses concerning the gods agreeably to the principles of theologists; rejecting indeed the tragical part of mythological fiction, but establishing first hypotheses in common with the authors of fables.

"Perhaps, however, some one may here object to us, that we do not in a proper manner exhibit the every where dispersed theology of Plato, and that we endeavour to heap together different particulars from different dialogues, as if we were studious of collecting many things into one mixture, instead of deriving them all from one and the same fountain. For if this were our intention, we might indeed refer different dogmas to different treatises of Plato, but we shall by no means have a precedaneous doctrine concerning the gods, nor will there be any dialogue which presents us with an all-perfect and entire procession of the divine genera, and their coordination with each other. But we shall be similar to those who endeavour to obtain a whole from parts, through the want of a whole prior to parts,[21] and to weave together the perfect, from things imperfect, when, on the contrary, the imperfect ought to have the first cause of its generation in the perfect. For the Timæus, for instance, will teach us the theory of the intelligible genera, and the Phædrus appears to present us with a regular account of the first intellectual orders. But where will be the coordination of intellectuals to intelligibles? And what will be the generation of second from first natures? In short, after what manner the progression of the divine orders takes place from the one principle of all things, and how in the generations of the gods, the orders between *the one*, and all-perfect number, are filled up, we shall be unable to evince.

"Farther still, it may be said, where will be the venerableness of your boasted science about divine natures? For it is absurd to call these dogmas, which are collected from many places, Platonic, and which, as you acknowledge, are introduced from foreign names to the philosophy of Plato; nor are you able to evince the whole entire truth about divine natures. Perhaps, indeed, they will say, that certain persons, junior to Plato, have delivered in their writings, and left to their disciples, one perfect form of philosophy. You, therefore, are able to produce one entire theory about nature from the Timæus; but from the Republic, or Laws, the most beautiful dogmas about morals, and which tend to one form of philosophy. Alone, therefore, neglecting the treatise of Plato, which contains all the good of the first philosophy, and which may be called the summit of the whole theory, you will be deprived of the most perfect knowledge of beings, unless you are so much infatuated, as to boast on account of fabulous fictions, though an analysis of things of this kind abounds with much of the probable, but not of the demonstrative. Besides, things of this kind are only delivered adventitiously in the Platonic dialogues; as the fable in the Protagoras, which is inserted for the sake of the political science, and the demonstrations respecting it. In like manner, the fable in the Republic is inserted for the sake of justice; and in the Gorgias for the sake of temperance. For Plato combines fabulous narrations with investigations of ethical dogmas, not for the sake of the fables, but for the sake of the leading design, that we may not only exercise the intellectual part of the soul, through contending reasons, but that the divine part of the soul may more perfectly receive the knowledge of beings, through its sympathy with more mystic concerns. For, from other discourses we resemble those who are compelled to the reception of truth; but from fables we are affected in an ineffable manner, and call forth our unperverted conceptions, venerating the mystic information which they contain.

"Hence, as it appears to me, Timæus with great propriety thinks it fit that we should produce the divine genera, following the inventors of fables as sons of the gods, and subscribe to their always generating secondary natures from such as are first, though they should speak without demonstration. For this kind of discourse is not demonstrative, but entheastic, or the progeny of divine inspiration; and was invented by the ancients, not through necessity, but for the sake of persuasion, not regarding naked discipline, but sympathy with things themselves. But if you are willing to speculate not only the causes of fables, but of other theological dogmas, you will find that some of them are scattered in the Platonic dialogues for the sake of ethical, and others for the sake of physical considerations. For in the Philebus, Plato discourses concerning bound and infinity, for the sake of pleasure, and a life according to intellect. For I think the latter are species of the former. In the Timæus, the discourse about the intelligible gods is assumed for the sake of the proposed physiology. On which account, it is every where necessary that images should be known from paradigms; but that the paradigms of material things should be immaterial, of sensibles intelligible, and of physical forms, separate from nature. But in the Phædrus, Plato celebrates the supercelestial place, the subcelestial profundity, and every genus under this for the sake of amatory mania; the manner in which the reminiscence of souls takes place; and the passage to these from hence. Every where, however, the leading end, as I may say, is either physical or political, while the conceptions about divine natures are introduced either for the sake of invention or perfection. How, therefore, can such a theory as yours be any longer venerable and supernatural, and worthy to be studied beyond every thing, when it is neither able to evince the whole in itself, nor the perfect, nor that which is precedaneous in the writings of Plato, but is destitute of all these, is violent and not spontaneous, and does not possess a genuine, but an adventitious order, as in a drama? And such are the particulars which may be urged against our design.

"To this objection I shall make a just and perspicuous reply. I say then that Plato every where discourses about the gods agreeably to ancient opinions and the nature of things. And sometimes indeed, for the sake of the cause of the things proposed, he reduces them to the principles of the dogmas, and thence, as from an exalted place of survey, contemplates the nature of the thing proposed. But sometimes he establishes the theological science as the leading end. For in the Phædrus, his subject respects intelligible beauty, and the participation of beauty pervading from thence through all things; and in the Banquet it respects the amatory order.

"But if it be necessary to consider, in one Platonic dialogue, the all-perfect, whole and connected, extending as far as to the complete number of theology, I shall perhaps assert a paradox, and which will alone be apparent to our familiars. We ought however to dare, since we have begun the assertions, and affirm against our opponents, that the Parmenides, and the mystic conceptions of this dialogue, will accomplish all you desire. For in this dialogue, all the divine genera proceed in order from the first cause, and evince their mutual suspension from each other. And those which are highest indeed, connate with *the one*, and of a primary nature, are allotted a form of subsistence characterized by unity, occult and simple; but such as are last, are multiplied, are distributed into many parts, and excel in number, but are inferior in power to such as are of a higher order; and such as are middle, according to a convenient proportion, are more composite than their causes, but more simple than their proper progeny. And in short, all the axioms of the theological science appear in perfection in this dialogue; and all the divine orders are exhibited subsisting in connection. So that this is nothing else than the celebrated generation of the gods, and the procession of every kind of being from the ineffable and unknown cause of wholes.[22] The Parmenides therefore enkindles in the lovers of Plato the whole and perfect light of the theological science. But after this, the aforementioned dialogues distribute parts of the mystic discipline about the gods, and all of them, as I may say, participate of divine wisdom, and excite our spontaneous conceptions respecting a divine nature. And it is necessary to refer all the parts of this mystic discipline to these dialogues, and these again to the one and all perfect theory of the Parmenides. For thus, as it appears to me, we shall suspend the more imperfect from the perfect, and parts from wholes, and shall exhibit reasons assimilated to things, of which, according to the Platonic Timæus, they are interpreters. Such then is our answer to the objection which may be urged against us; and thus we refer the Platonic theory to the Parmenides; just as the Timæus is acknowledged by all who are in the least degree intelligent, to contain the whole science about nature."

All that is here asserted by Proclus will be immediately admitted by the reader who understands the outlines which we have here given of the theology of Plato, and who is besides this a complete master of the mystic meaning of the Parmenides; which I trust he will find sufficiently unfolded, through the assistance of Proclus, in my introduction and notes to that dialogue.

The next important Platonic dogma in order, is that concerning ideas, about which the reader will find so much said in the notes on the Parmenides, that but little remains to be added here. That little however is as follows: The divine Pythagoras, and all those who have legitimately received his doctrines, among whom Plato holds the most distinguished rank, asserted that there are many orders of beings, *viz.* intelligible, intellectual, dianoëtic, physical, or, in short, vital and corporeal essences. For the progression of things, the subjection which naturally subsists together with such progression, and the power of diversity in coordinate genera, give subsistence to all the multitude of corporeal and incorporeal natures. They said, therefore, that there are three orders in the whole extent of beings, *viz.* the *intelligible*, the *dianoëtic*, and the *sensible;* and that in each of these ideas subsist, characterized by the respective essential properties of the natures by which they are contained. And with respect to intelligible ideas, these they placed among divine natures, together with the producing, paradigmatic, and final causes of things in a consequent order. For if these three causes sometimes concur, and are united among themselves (which Aristotle says is the case), without doubt this will not happen in the lowest works of nature, but in the first and most excellent causes of all things, which on account of their exuberant fecundity have a power generative of all things, and from their converting and rendering similar to themselves the natures which they have generated, are the paradigms or exemplars of all things. But as these divine causes act for their own sake, and on account of their own goodness, do they not exhibit the final cause? Since therefore intelligible forms are of this kind, and are the leaders of so much good to wholes, they give completion to the divine orders, though they largely subsist about the intelligible order contained in the artificer of the universe. But dianoëtic forms or ideas imitate the intellectual, which have a prior subsistence, render the order of soul similar to the intellectual order, and comprehend all things in a secondary degree.

These forms beheld in divine natures possess a fabricative power, but with us they are only gnostic, and no longer demiurgic, through the defluxion of our wings, or degradation of our intellectual powers. For, as Plato says in the Phædrus, when the winged powers of the soul are perfect and plumed for flight, she dwells on high, and in conjunction with divine natures governs the world. In the Timæus, he manifestly asserts that the demiurgus implanted these dianoëtic forms in souls, in geometric, arithmetic, and harmonic proportions: but in his Republic (in the section of a line in the 6th book) he calls them images of intelligibles; and on this account does not for the most part disdain to denominate them intellectual, as being the exemplars of sensible natures. In the Phædo he says that these are the causes to us of reminiscence; because disciplines are nothing else than reminiscences of middle dianoëtic forms, from which the productive powers of nature being derived, and inspired, give birth to all the mundane phænomena.

Plato however did not consider things definable, or in modern language abstract ideas, as the only universals, but prior to these he established those principles productive of science which essentially reside in the soul, as is evident from his Phædrus and Phædo. In the 10th book of the Republic too, he venerates those separate forms which subsist in a divine intellect. In the Phædrus, he asserts that souls, elevated to the supercelestial place, behold justice herself, temperance herself, and science herself; and lastly in the Phædo he evinces the immortality of the soul from the hypothesis of separate forms.

Syrianus,[23] in his commentary on the 13th book of Aristotle's Metaphysics, shows, in defence of Socrates, Plato, the Parmenidæans, and Pythagoreans, that ideas were not introduced by these divine men, according to the usual meaning of names, as was the opinion of Chrysippus, Archedemus, and many of the junior Stoics; for ideas are distinguished by many differences, from things which are denominated from custom. Nor do they subsist, says he, together with intellect, in the same manner as those slender conceptions which are denominated universals abstracted from sensibles, according to the hypothesis of Longinus:[24] for if that which subsists is unsubstantial, it cannot be consubsistent with intellect. Nor are ideas according to these men *notions*, as Cleanthes afterwards asserted them to be. Nor is idea definitive reason, nor material form: for these subsist in composition and division, and verge to matter. But ideas are perfect, simple, immaterial, and impartible natures. And what wonder is there, says Syrianus, if we should separate things which are so much distant from each other? Since neither do we imitate in this particular Plutarch, Atticus, and Democritus, who, because universal reasons perpetually subsist in the essence of the soul, were of opinion that these reasons are ideas: for though they separate them from the universal in sensible natures, yet it is not proper to conjoin in one and the same, the reasons of soul, and an intellect such as ours, with paradigmatic and immaterial forms, and demiurgic intellections. But as the divine Plato says, it is the province of our soul to collect things into one by a reasoning process, and to possess a reminiscence of those transcendent spectacles, which we once beheld when governing the universe in conjunction with divinity. Boethus,[25] the peripatetic too, with whom it is proper to join Cornutus, thought that ideas are the same with universals in sensible natures. However, whether these universals are prior to particulars, they are not prior in such a manner as to be denudated from the habitude which they possess with respect to them, nor do they subsist as the causes of particulars; both which are the prerogatives of ideas: or whether they are posterior to particulars, as many are accustomed to call them, how can things of posterior origin, which have no essential subsistence, but are nothing more than slender conceptions, sustain the dignity of fabricative ideas?

In what manner then, says Syrianus, do ideas subsist according to the contemplative lovers of truth? We reply, intelligibly and tetradically (νοητως και τετραδικως), in *animal itself* (εν τω αυτοζωω), or the extremity of the intelligible order;[26] but intellectually and decadically (νοερως και δεκαδικως), in the intellect of the artificer of the universe: for, according to the Pythagoric Hymn:

> "Divine number proceeds from the retreats of the undecaying monad, till it arrives at the divine tetrad which produced the mother of all things, the universal recipient, venerable, circularly

investing all things with bound, immovable and unwearied, and which is denominated the sacred decad, both by the immortal gods and earthborn men." προεισι γαρ ο θειος αριθμος, ως φησιν ο Πυθαγορειος εις αυτον υμνος,

Μοναδος εκ κευθμωνος ακηρατου εστ' αν ικηται
Τετραδα επι ζαθεην, ἡ δη τεκε μητερα παντων
Πανδεχεα, πρεσβειραν, ορον περι πασι τιθεισαν,
Ατροπον, ακαματον, δεκαδα κλειουσι μιν αγνην
Αθανατοι τε θεοι και γηγενεεις ανθρωποι.

And such is the mode of their subsistence according to Orpheus, Pythagoras, and Plato. Or if it be requisite to speak in more familiar language, an intellect sufficient to itself, and which is a most perfect cause, presides over the wholes of the universe, and through these governs all its parts; but at the same time that it fabricates all mundane natures, and benefits them by its providential energies, it preserves its own most divine and immaculate purity; and while it illuminates all things, is not mingled with the natures which it illuminates. This intellect, therefore, comprehending in the depths of its essence an ideal world, replete with all various forms, excludes privation of cause, and casual subsistence, from its energy. But as it imparts every good and all possible beauty to its fabrications, it converts the universe to itself, and renders it similar to its own omniform nature. Its energy, too, is such as its intellection; but it understands all things, since it is most perfect. Hence there is not any thing which ranks among true beings, that is not comprehended in the essence of intellect; but it always establishes in itself ideas, which are not different from itself and its essence but give completion to it, and introduce to the whole of things a cause which is at the same time productive, paradigmatic, and final. For it energizes as intellect, and the ideas which it contains are paradigmatic, as being forms; and they energize from themselves, and according to their own exuberant goodness. And such are the Platonic dogmas concerning ideas, which sophistry and ignorance may indeed oppose, but will never be able to confute.

From this intelligible world, replete with omniform ideas, this sensible world, according to Plato, perpetually flows, depending on its artificer intellect, in the same manner as shadow on its forming substance. For as a deity of an intellectual characteristic is its fabricator, and both the essence and energy of intellect are established in eternity, the sensible universe, which is the effect or production of such an energy, must be consubsistent with its cause, or, in other words, must be a perpetual emanation from it. This will be evident from considering, that every thing which is generated, is either generated by art, or by nature, or according to power. It is necessary, therefore, that every thing operating according to nature or art should be prior to the things produced; but that things operating according to power should have their productions coexistent with themselves; just as the sun produces light coexistent with itself; fire, heat; and snow, coldness. If therefore the artificer of the universe produced it by art, he would not cause it simply to be, but to be in some particular manner; for all art produces form. Whence therefore does the world derive its being? If he produced it from nature, since that which makes by nature imparts something of itself to its productions, and the maker of the world is incorporeal, it would be necessary that the world, the offspring of such an energy, should be incorporeal. It remains, therefore, that the demiurgus produced the universe by power alone; but every thing generated by power subsists together with the cause containing this power: and hence productions of this kind cannot be destroyed, unless the producing cause is deprived of power. The divine intellect therefore that produced the sensible universe caused it to be coexistent with himself.

This world thus depending on its divine artificer, who is himself an intelligible world, replete with the archetypal ideas of all things, considered according to its corporeal nature, is perpetually flowing, and perpetually advancing to being (εν τῳ γιγνεσθοει), and compared with its paradigm, has no stability or reality of being. However, considered as animated by a divine soul, and as receiving the illuminations of all the supermundane gods, and being itself the receptacle of divinities from whom bodies are suspended, it is said by Plato in the Timæus to be a blessed god. The great body of this world too, which subsists in a perpetual dispersion of temporal extension, may be properly called *a whole with a total subsistence*, on account of the perpetuity of its duration, though this is nothing more than a flowing eternity. And hence Plato calls it *a whole of wholes;* by the other wholes which are comprehended in it meaning, the celestial spheres, the sphere of fire, the whole of air considered as one great orb; the whole earth, and the whole sea. These spheres, which are called by Platonic writers, *parts with a total subsistence*, are considered by Plato as aggregately perpetual. For if the body of the world is perpetual, this also must be the case with its larger parts, on account of their exquisite alliance to it, and in order that *wholes with a partial* subsistence, such as all individuals, may rank in the last gradation of things.

As the world too, considered as one great comprehending whole, is called by Plato a divine animal, so likewise every whole which it contains is a world, possessing, in the first place, a self-perfect unity; proceeding from the ineffable, by which it becomes a god; in the second place, a divine intellect; in the third place, a divine soul; and in the last place, a deified body. Hence each of these wholes is the producing cause of all the multitude which it contains, and on this account is said to be a whole prior to parts; because, considered as possessing an eternal form which holds all its parts together, and gives to the whole perpetuity of subsistence, it is not indigent of such parts to the perfection of its being. That these wholes which rank thus high in the universe are animated, must follow by a geometrical necessity. For, as Theophrastus well observes, wholes would possess less authority than parts, and things eternal than such as are corruptible, if deprived of the possession of soul.

And now having with venturous, yet unpresuming wing, ascended to the ineffable principle of things, and standing with every eye closed in the vestibules of the adytum, found that we could announce nothing concerning him, but only indicate our doubts and disappointment, and having thence descended to his occult and most venerable progeny, and passing through the luminous world of ideas, holding fast by the golden chain of deity, terminated our downward flight in the material universe, and its undecaying wholes, let us stop awhile and contemplate the sublimity and magnificence of the scene which this journey presents to our view. Here then we see the vast empire of deity, an empire terminated upwards by a principle so ineffable that all language is subverted about it, and downwards by the vast body of the world. Immediately subsisting after this immense unknown, we in the next place behold a mighty all-comprehending one, which, as being next to that which is in every respect incomprehensible, possesses much of the ineffable and unknown. From this principle of principles, in which all things causally subsist absorbed in superessential light and involved in unfathomable depths, we view a beauteous progeny of principles, all largely partaking of the ineffable, all stamped with the occult characters of deity, all possessing an overflowing fullness of good. From these dazzling summits, these ineffable blossoms, these divine propagations, we next see being, life, intellect, soul, nature and body depending; *monads* suspended from *unities*, deified natures proceeding from deities. Each of these monads too, is the leader of a series which extends from itself to the last of things, and which while it proceeds from, at the same time abides in, and returns to its leader. And all these principles and all their progeny are finally centred and rooted by their summits in the first great all-comprehending one. Thus all beings proceed from, and are comprehended in the first being; all intellects emanate from one first intellect; all souls from one first soul; all natures blossom from one first nature; and all bodies proceed from the vital and luminous body of the world. And lastly, all these great monads are comprehended in the first one, from which both they and all their depending series are unfolded into light. Hence this first one is truly the unity of unities, the monad of monads, the principle of principles, the God of gods, one and all things, and yet one prior to all.

Such, according to Plato, are the flights of the true philosopher, such the august and magnificent scene which presents itself to his view. By ascending these luminous heights, the spontaneous tendencies of the soul to deity alone find the adequate object of their desire; investigation here alone finally reposes, doubt expires in certainty, and knowledge loses itself in the ineffable.

And here perhaps some grave objector, whose little soul is indeed acute, but sees nothing with a vision healthy and sound, will say that all this is very magnificent, but that it is soaring too high for man; that it is merely the effect of spiritual pride; that no truths, either in morality or theology, are of any importance which are not adapted to the level of the meanest capacity; and that all that it is necessary for man to know concerning either God or himself is so plain, that he that runs may read. In answer to such like cant, for it is nothing more,—a cant produced by the most profound ignorance, and frequently attended with the most deplorable envy, I ask, is then the Delphic precept, KNOW THYSELF, a trivial mandate? Can this be accomplished by every man? Or can any one properly know himself without knowing the rank he holds in the scale of being? And can this be effected without knowing what are the natures which he surpasses, and what those are by which he is surpassed? And can he know this without knowing as much of those natures as it is possible for him to know? And will the objector be hardy enough to say that every man is equal to this arduous task? That he who rushes from the forge, or the mines, with a soul distorted, crushed and bruised by base mechanical arts, and madly presumes to teach theology to a deluded audience, is master of this sublime, this most important science? For my own part I know of no truths which are thus obvious, thus accessible to every man, but axioms, those self-evident principles of science which are conspicuous by their own light, which are the spontaneous unperverted conceptions of the soul, and to which he who does not assent deserves, as Aristotle justly remarks, either pity or correction. In short, if this is to be the criterion of all moral and theological knowledge, that it must be immediately obvious to every man, that it is to be apprehended by the most careless inspection, what occasion is there for seminaries of learning? Education is ridiculous, the toil of investigation is idle. Let us at once confine Wisdom in the dungeons of Folly, recall Ignorance from her barbarous wilds, and close the gates of Science with everlasting bars.

Having thus taken a general survey of the great world, and descended from the intelligible to the sensible universe, let us still, adhering to that golden chain which is bound round the summit of Olympus, and from which all things are suspended, descend to the microcosm man. For man comprehends in himself partially every thing which the world contains divinely and totally. Hence, according to Plato, he is endued with an intellect subsisting in energy, and a rational soul proceeding from the same father and vivific goddess as were the causes of the intellect and soul of the universe. He has likewise an ethereal vehicle analogous to the heavens, and a terrestrial body composed from the four elements, and with which also it is coordinate.

With respect to his rational part, for in this the essence of man consists, we have already shown that it is of a self-motive nature, and that it subsists between intellect, which is immovable both in essence and energy, and nature, which both moves and is moved. In consequence of this middle subsistence, the mundane soul, from which all partial souls are derived, is said by Plato, in the Timæus, to be a medium between that which is indivisible and that which is divisible about bodies, *i.e.* the mundane soul is a medium between the mundane intellect, and the whole of that corporeal life which the world participates. In like manner the human soul is a medium between a dæmoniacal intellect proximately established above our essence, which it also elevates and perfects, and that corporeal life which is distributed about our body, and which is the cause of its generation, nutrition, and increase. This dæmoniacal intellect is called by Plato, in the Phædrus, *theoretic* and *the governor of the soul.* The highest part therefore of the human soul is the summit of the dianoëtic power (το ακροτατον της διανοιας), or that power which reasons scientifically; and this summit is our intellect. As, however, our very essence is characterized by reason, this our summit is rational, and though it subsists in energy, yet it has a remitted union with things themselves. Though too it energizes from itself, and contains intelligibles in its essence, yet from its alliance to the discursive nature of soul, and its inclination to that which is divisible, it falls short of the perfection of an intellectual essence and energy profoundly indivisible and united, and the intelligibles which it contains degenerate from the transcendently fulged and self-luminous nature of first intelligibles. Hence, in obtaining a perfectly indivisible knowledge, it requires to be perfected by an intellect whose energy is ever vigilant and unremitted; and its intelligibles, that they may become perfect, are indigent of the light which proceeds from separate intelligibles. Aristotle, therefore, very properly compares the intelligibles of our intellect to colours, because these require the splendour of the sun, and denominates an intellect of this kind, *intellect in capacity*, both on account of its subordination to an essential intellect, and because it is from a separate intellect that it receives the full perfection of its nature. The middle part of the rational soul is called by Plato *dianoia* (διανοια), and is that power which, as we have already said, reasons scientifically, deriving the principles of its reasoning, which are axioms, from intellect. And the extremity of the rational soul is *opinion*, which in his Sophista he defines to be that power which knows the conclusion of *dianoia*. This power also knows the universal in sensible particulars, as that every man is a biped, but it knows only the οτι, or *that* a thing is, but is ignorant of the διοτι, or *why* it is: knowledge of the latter kind being the province of the dianoëtic power.

And such is Plato's division of the rational part of our nature, which he very justly considers as the *true man;* the essence of every thing consisting in its most excellent part.

After this follows the irrational nature, the summit of which is the phantasy, or that power which perceives every thing accompanied with figure and interval; and on this account it may be called *a figured intelligence* (μορφωτικη νοησις). This power, as Iamblichus beautifully observes, grows upon, as it were, and fashions all the powers of the soul; exciting in opinion the illuminations from the senses, and fixing in that life which is extended with body, the impressions which descend from intellect. Hence, says Proclus, it folds itself about the indivisibility of true intellect, conforms itself to all formless species, and becomes perfectly every thing, from which the dianoëtic power, and our indivisible reason consists. Hence too, it is all things passively which intellect is impassively, and on this account Aristotle calls it passive intellect. Under this subsist anger and desire, the former resembling a raging lion, and the latter a many-headed beast; and the whole is bounded by sense, which is nothing more than a passive perception of things, and on this account is justly said by Plato to be rather *passion* than *knowledge;* since the former of these is characterized by *inertness*, and the latter by *energy*.

Further still, in order that the union of the soul with this gross terrestrial body may be effected in a becoming manner, two vehicles, according to Plato, are necessary as media, one of which is ethereal, and the other aerial, and of these, the ethereal vehicle is *simple and immaterial;* and this dense earthly body is *composite and material.*

The soul thus subsisting as a medium between natures impartible and such as are divided about bodies, it produces and constitutes the latter of these; but establishes in itself the prior causes from which it proceeds. Hence it previously receives, after the manner of an exemplar, the natures to which it is prior as their cause; but it possesses through participation, and as the blossoms of first natures, the causes of its subsistence. Hence it contains in its essence immaterial forms of things material, incorporeal of such as are corporeal, and unextended of such as are distinguished by interval. But it contains intelligibles after the manner of an image, and receives partibly their impartible forms, such as are uniform variously, and such as are immovable, according to a self-motive condition. Soul therefore is all things, and is elegantly said by Olympiodorus to be an *omniform statue* (παμμορφον αγαλμα): for it contains such things as are first through participation, but such as are posterior to its nature, after the manner of an exemplar.

As, too, it is *always* moved, and this *always* is not eternal, but temporal, for that which is properly eternal, and such is intellect, is perfectly stable, and has no transitive energies,—hence it is necessary that its motions should be periodic. For motion is a certain mutation from some things into others. And beings are terminated by multitudes and magnitudes. These therefore being terminated, there can neither be an infinite mutation, according to a right line, nor can that which is always moved proceed according to a finished progression. Hence that which is always moved will proceed from the same to the same; and will thus form a periodic motion. Hence, too, the human, and this also is true of every mundane soul, uses periods and restitutions of its proper life. For, in consequence of being measured by time, it energizes transitively, and possesses a proper motion. But every thing which is moved perpetually and participates of time, revolves periodically and proceeds from the same to the same. And hence the soul, from possessing motion and energizing according to time, will both possess periods of motion, and restitutions to its pristine state.

Again, as the human soul, according to Plato, ranks among the number of those souls that *sometimes* follow the mundane divinities, in consequence of subsisting immediately after dæmons and heroes, the *perpetual* attendants of the gods, hence it possesses a power of descending infinitely into generation, or the sublunary region, and of ascending from generation to real being. For since it does not reside with divinity through an infinite time, neither will it be conversant with bodies through the whole succeeding time. For that which has no temporal beginning, both according to Plato and Aristotle, cannot have an end; and that which has no end, is necessarily without a beginning. It remains, therefore, that every soul must perform periods, both of ascensions from generation, and of descensions into generation; and that this will never fail, through an infinite time.

From all this it follows that the soul, while an inhabitant of earth, is in a fallen condition, an apostate from deity, an exile from the orb of light. Hence Plato, in the 7th book of his Republic, considering our life with reference to erudition and the want of it, assimilates us to men in a subterranean cavern, who have been there confined from their childhood, and so fettered by chains as to be only able to look before them to the entrance of the cave which expands to the light, but incapable through the chain of turning themselves round. He supposes too, that they have the light of a fire burning far above and behind them; and that between the fire and the fettered men, there is a road above, along which a low wall is built. On this wall are seen men bearing utensils of every kind, and statues in wood and stone of men and other animals. And of these men some are speaking and others silent. With respect to the fettered men in this cave, they see nothing of themselves or another, or of what is carrying along, but the shadows formed by the fire falling on the opposite part of the cave. He supposes too, that the opposite part of this prison has an echo; and that in consequence of this the fettered men, when they hear any one speak, will imagine that it is nothing else than the passing shadow.

Here, in the first place, as we have observed in the notes on that book, the road above, between the fire and the fettered men, indicates that there is a certain ascent in the cave itself from a more abject to a more elevated life. By this ascent therefore Plato signifies the contemplation of dianoëtic objects, in the mathematical disciplines. For as the shadows in the cave correspond to the shadows of visible objects, and visible objects are the immediate images of dianoëtic forms, or those ideas which the soul essentially participates, it is evident that the objects from which these shadows are formed must correspond to such as are dianoëtic. It is requisite, therefore, that the dianoëtic power, exercising itself in these, should draw forth the principles of these from their latent retreats, and should contemplate them not in images, but as subsisting in herself in impartible involution.

In the next place he says, that:

> "the man who is to be led from the cave, will more easily see what the heavens contain, and the heavens themselves, by looking in the night to the light of the stars, and the moon, than by day looking on the sun, and the light of the sun."

By this he signifies the contemplation of intelligibles: for the stars and their light are imitations of intelligibles, so far as all of them partake of the form of the sun, in the same manner as intelligibles are characterized by the nature of *the good*.

After the contemplation of these, and after the eye is accustomed through these to the light, as it is requisite in the visible region to see the sun himself in the last place, in like manner, according to Plato, the idea of *the good* must be seen the last in the intelligible region. He likewise divinely adds, *that it is scarcely to be seen;* for we can only be conjoined with it through the intelligible, in the vestibule of which it is beheld by the ascending soul.

In short, the soul, according to Plato, can only be restored while on earth to the divine likeness, which she abandoned by her descent, and be able after death to reascend to the intelligible world, by the exercise of the cathartic and theoretic[27] virtues; the former purifying her from the defilements of a mortal nature, and the latter elevating her to the vision of true being: for thus, as Plato says in the Timæus:

> "the soul becoming sane and entire, will arrive at the form of her pristine habit."[28]

The cathartic, however, must necessarily precede the theoretic virtues; since it is impossible to survey truth while subject to the perturbation and tumult of the passions. For the rational soul subsisting as a medium between intellect and the irrational nature, can then only without divulsion associate with the intellect prior to herself, when she becomes pure from copassivity with inferior natures. By the cathartic virtues, therefore, we become *sane*, in consequence of being liberated from the passions as diseases; but we become *entire* by the reassumption of intellect and science, as of our proper parts; and this is effected by contemplative truth. Plato also clearly teaches us that our apostasy from better natures is only to be healed by a flight from hence, when he defines in his Theætetus philosophy to be a flight from terrestrial evils: for he evinces by this that passions are connascent with mortals alone. He likewise says in the same dialogue, that:

> "neither can evils be abolished, nor yet do they subsist with the gods, but that they necessarily revolve about this terrene abode, and a mortal nature."

For those who are obnoxious to generation and corruption can also be affected in a manner contrary to nature, which is the beginning of evils. But in the same dialogue he subjoins the mode by which our flight from evil is to be accomplished.

> "It is necessary," says he, "to fly from hence thither: but the flight is a similitude to divinity, as far as is possible to man; and this similitude consists in becoming just and holy in conjunction with intellectual prudence."[29]

For it is necessary that he who wishes to run from evils, should in the first place turn away from a mortal nature; since it is not possible for those who are mingled with it to avoid being filled with its attendant evils. As therefore, through our flight from divinity, and the defluxion of those wings which elevate us on high, we fell into this mortal abode, and thus became connected with evils, so by abandoning passivity with a mortal nature, and by the germination of the virtues, as of certain wings, we return to the abode of pure and true good, and to the possession of divine felicity. For the essence of man subsisting as a medium between dæmoniacal natures, who always have an intellectual knowledge of divinity, and those beings who are never adapted by nature to understand him, it ascends to the former and descends to the latter, through the possession and desertion of intellect. For it becomes familiar both with the divine and brutal likeness, through the amphibious condition of its nature.

When the soul therefore has recovered her pristine perfection in as great a degree as is possible, while she is an inhabitant of earth by the exercise of the cathartic and theoretic virtues, she returns after death, as he says in the Timæus, to her kindred star from which she fell, and enjoys a blessed life. Then too, as he says in the Phædrus, being winged, she governs the world in conjunction with the gods. And this indeed is the most beautiful end of her labours. This is what he calls in the Phædo, a great contest, and a mighty hope.[30] This is the most perfect fruit of philosophy to familiarize and lead her back to things truly beautiful, to liberate her from this terrene abode as from a certain subterranean cavern of material life, elevate her to ethereal splendours, and place her in the islands of the blessed.

From this account of the human soul, that most important Platonic dogma necessarily follows, that our soul essentially contains all knowledge, and that whatever knowledge she acquires in the present life, is in reality nothing more than a recovery of what she once possessed. This recovery is very properly called by Plato reminiscence, not as being attended with actual recollection in the present life, but as being an actual repossession of what the soul had lost through her oblivious union with the body. Alluding to this essential knowledge of the soul, which discipline evocates from its dormant retreats, Plato says, in the Sophista, that "we know all things as in a dream, and are again ignorant of them, according to vigilant perception." Hence too, as Proclus[31] well observes, it is evident that the soul does not collect her knowledge from sensibles, nor from things partial and divisible discover *the whole* and *the one*. For it is not proper to think that things which have in no respect a real subsistence, should be the leading causes of knowledge to the soul; and that things which oppose each other and are ambiguous, should precede science which has a sameness of subsistence; nor that things which are variously mutable should be generative of reasons which are established in unity; nor that things indefinite should be the causes of definite intelligence. It is not fit, therefore, that the truth of things eternal should be received from *the many*, nor the discrimination of universals from sensibles, nor a judgment respecting what is good from irrational natures; but it is requisite, that the soul entering within herself, should investigate in herself *the true* and *the good*, and the eternal reasons of things.

We have said that discipline awakens the dormant knowledge of the soul; and Plato considered this as particularly effected by the mathematical disciplines. Hence he asserts of theoretic arithmetic, that it imparts no small aid to our ascent to real being, and that it liberates us from the wandering and ignorance about a sensible nature. Geometry too is considered by him as most instrumental to the knowledge of *the good*, when it is not pursued for the sake of practical purposes, but as the means of ascent to an intelligible essence. Astronomy also is useful for the purpose of investigating the fabricator of all things, and contemplating as in most splendid images the ideal world, and its ineffable cause. And lastly music, when properly studied, is subservient to our ascent, *viz.* when from sensible we betake ourselves to the contemplation of ideal and divine harmony. Unless, however, we thus employ the mathematical disciplines, the study of them is justly considered by Plato as imperfect and useless, and of no worth. For as the true end of man according to his philosophy is an assimilation to divinity, in the greatest perfection of which human nature is capable, whatever contributes to this, is to be ardently pursued; but whatever has a different tendency, however necessary it may be to the wants and conveniences of the mere animal life, is comparatively little and vile. Hence it is necessary to pass rapidly from things visible and audible, to those which are alone seen by the eye of intellect. For the mathematical sciences, when properly studied, move the inherent knowledge of the soul; awaken its intelligence; purify its dianoëtic power; call forth its essential forms from their dormant retreats; remove that oblivion and ignorance which are congenial with our birth; and dissolve the bonds arising from our union with an irrational nature. It is therefore beautifully said by Plato, in the 7th book of his Republic, that:

> "the soul through these disciplines has an organ purified and enlightened, which is blinded and buried by studies of a different kind, an organ better worth saving than ten thousand eyes, since truth becomes visible through this alone."

Dialectic, however, or the vertex of the mathematical sciences, as it is called by Plato in his Republic, is that master discipline which particularly leads us up to an intelligible essence. Of this first of sciences, which is essentially different from vulgar logic, and is the same with what Aristotle calls the first philosophy and wisdom, I have largely spoken in the introduction and notes to the Parmenides. Suffice it therefore to observe in this place, that dialectic differs from mathematical science in this, that the latter flows from, and the former is void of hypothesis. That dialectic has a power of knowing universals; that it ascends to good and the supreme cause of all; and that it considers good as the end of its elevation; but that the mathematical science, which previously fabricates for itself definite principles, from which it evinces things consequent to such principles, does not tend to the principle, but to the conclusion. Hence Plato does not expel mathematical knowledge from the number of the sciences, but asserts it to be the next in rank to that one science which is the summit of all; nor does he accuse it as ignorant of its own principles, but considers it as receiving these from the master science dialectic, and that possessing them without any demonstration, it demonstrates from these its consequent propositions.

Hence Socrates, in the Republic, speaking of the power of dialectic, says, that it surrounds all disciplines like a defensive enclosure, and elevates those that use it, to the good itself, and the first unities; that it purifies the eye of the soul; establishes itself in true beings, and the one principle of all things, and ends at last in that which is no longer hypothetical. The power of dialectic, therefore, being thus great, and the end of this path so mighty, it must by no means be confounded with arguments which are alone conversant with opinion: for the former is the guardian of sciences, and the passage to it is through these, but the latter is perfectly destitute of disciplinative science. To which we may add, that the method of reasoning, which is founded in opinion, regards only that which is apparent; but the dialectic method endeavours to arrive at *the one* itself, always employing for this purpose steps of ascent, and at last beautifully ends in the nature of *the good*. Very different, therefore, is it from the merely logical method, which presides over the demonstrative phantasy, is of a secondary nature, and is alone pleased with contentious discussions. For the dialectic of Plato for the most part employs divisions and analyses as primary sciences, and as imitating the progression of beings from *the one*, and their conversion to it again. It likewise sometimes uses definitions and demonstrations, and prior to these the definitive method, and the divisive prior to this. On the contrary, the merely logical method, which is solely conversant with opinion, is deprived of the incontrovertible reasonings of demonstration.

The following is a specimen of the analytical method of Plato's dialectic.[32] Of analysis there are three species. For one is an ascent from sensibles to the first intelligibles; a second is an ascent through things demonstrated and subdemonstrated, to undemonstrated and immediate propositions; and a third proceeds from hypothesis to unhypothetical principles. Of the first of these species, Plato has given a most admirable specimen in the speech of Diotima in the Banquet. For there he ascends from the beauty about bodies to the beauty in souls; from this to the beauty in right disciplines; from this again to the beauty in laws; from the beauty in laws to the ample sea of beauty (το πολυ πελαγος του καλου); and thus proceeding, he at length arrives at the beautiful itself.

The second species of analysis is as follows: It is necessary to make the thing investigated, the subject of hypothesis; to survey such things as are prior to it; and to demonstrate these from things posterior, ascending to such as are prior, till we arrive at the first thing, and to which we give our assent. But beginning from this, we descend synthetically to the thing investigated. Of this species, the following is an example, from the Phædrus of Plato. It is inquired if the soul is immortal; and this being hypothetically admitted, it is inquired in the next place if it is always moved. This being demonstrated, the next inquiry is, if that which is always moved, is self-moved; and this again being demonstrated, it is considered whether that which is self-moved, is the principle of motion; and afterwards if the principle is unbegotten. This then being admitted as a thing acknowledged, and likewise that what is unbegotten is incorruptible, the demonstration of the thing proposed is thus collected. If there is a principle, it is unbegotten and incorruptible. That which is self-moved is the principle of motion. Soul is self-moved. Soul therefore (*i.e.* the rational soul) is incorruptible, unbegotten, and immortal.

Of the third species of analysis, which proceeds from the hypothetical to that which is unhypothetic, Plato has given a most beautiful specimen in the first hypothesis of his Parmenides. For here, taking for his hypothesis that *the one is*, he proceeds through an orderly series of negations, which are not privative of their subjects, but generative of things which are as it were their opposites, till he at length takes away the hypothesis, that *the one is*. For he denies of it all discourse and every appellation. And thus evidently denies of it not only that it *is*, but even negation. For all things are posterior to *the one; viz.* things known, knowledge, and the instruments of knowledge. And thus, beginning from the hypothetical, he ends in that which is unhypothetical, and truly ineffable.

Having taken a general survey, both of the great world and the microcosm man, I shall close this account of the principal dogmas of Plato, with the outlines of his doctrine concerning Providence and Fate, as it is a subject of the greatest importance, and the difficulties in which it is involved are happily removed by that prince of philosophers.[33]

In the first place, therefore, Providence, according to common conceptions, is the cause of good to the subjects of its care; and Fate is the cause of a certain connection to generated natures. This being admitted, let us consider what the things are which are connected. Of beings, therefore, some have their essence in eternity, and others in time. But by beings whose essence is in eternity, I mean those whose energy as well as their essence is eternal; and by beings essentially temporal, those whose essence is always in generation, or becoming to be, though this should take place in an infinite time. The media between these two extremes are natures, which, in a certain respect, have an essence permanent and better than generation, or a flowing subsistence, but whose energy is measured by time. For it is necessary that every procession from things first to last should be effected through media. The medium, therefore, between these two extremes, must either be that which has an eternal essence, but an energy indigent of time, or, on the contrary, that which has a temporal essence, but an eternal energy. It is impossible, however, for the latter of these to have any subsistence; for if this were admitted, energy would be prior to essence. The medium, therefore, must be that whose essence is eternal, but energy temporal. And the three orders which compose this first middle and last are, the intellectual, psychical (or that pertaining to soul), and corporeal. For from what has been already said by us concerning the gradation of beings, it is evident that the intellectual order is established in eternity, both in essence and energy; that the corporeal order is always in generation, or advancing to being, and this either in an infinite time, or in a part of time; and that the psychical is indeed eternal in essence, but temporal in energy. Where then shall we rank things which, being distributed either in places or times, have a certain coordination and sympathy with each other through connection? It is evident that they must be ranked among altermotive and corporeal natures. For of things which subsist beyond the order of bodies, some are better both than place and time; and others, though they energize according to time, appear to be entirely pure from any connection with place.

Hence things which are governed and connected by Fate are entirely altermotive and corporeal. If this then is demonstrated, it is manifest, that admitting Fate to be a cause of connection, we must assert that it presides over altermotive and corporeal natures. If, therefore, we look to that which is the proximate cause of bodies, and through which also altermotive beings are moved, breathe, and are held together, we shall find that this is nature, the energies of which are to generate, nourish, and increase. If, therefore, this power not only subsists in us and all other animals and plants, but prior to partial bodies there is, by a much greater necessity, one nature of the world which comprehends and is motive of all bodies; it follows, that nature must be the cause of things connected, and that in this we must investigate Fate. Hence Fate is nature, or that incorporeal power which is the one life of the world, presiding over bodies, moving all things according to time, and connecting the motions of things that, by places and times, are distant from each other. It is likewise the cause of the mutual sympathy of mortal natures, and of their conjunction with such as are eternal. For the nature which is in us, binds and connects all the parts of our body, of which also it is a certain Fate. And as in our body some parts have a principal subsistence, and others are less principal, and the latter are consequent to the former, so in the universe, the generations of the less principal parts are consequent to the motions of the more principal, *viz.* the sublunary generations to the periods of the celestial bodies; and the circle of the former is the image of the latter.

Hence it is not difficult to see that Providence is deity itself, the fountain of all good. For whence can good be imparted to all things, but from divinity? So that no other cause of good but deity is, as Plato says, to be assigned. And, in the next place, as this cause is superior to all intelligible and sensible natures, it is consequently superior to Fate. Whatever too is subject to Fate, is also under the dominion of Providence; having its connection indeed from Fate, but deriving the good which it possesses from Providence. But again, not all things that are under the dominion of Providence are indigent of Fate; for intelligibles are exempt from its sway. Fate therefore is profoundly conversant with corporeal natures; since connection introduces time and corporeal motion. Hence Plato, looking to this, says in the Timæus, that the world is mingled from intellect and necessity, the former ruling over the latter. For by necessity here he means the motive cause of bodies, which in other places he calls Fate. And this with great propriety; since every body is compelled to do whatever it does, and to suffer whatever it suffers; to heat or to be heated, to impart or to receive cold. But the elective power is unknown to a corporeal nature; so that the necessary and the nonelective may be said to be the peculiarities of bodies.

As there are two genera of things therefore, the intelligible and the sensible, so likewise there are two kingdoms of these; that of Providence upwards, which reigns over intelligibles and sensibles, and that of Fate downwards, which reigns over sensibles only. Providence likewise differs from Fate, in the same manner as deity, from that which is divine indeed, but by participation, and not primarily. For in other things we see that which has a primary subsistence, and that which subsists according to participation. Thus the light which subsists in the orb of the sun is primary light, and that which is in the air, according to participation; the latter being derived from the former. And life is primarily in the soul, but secondarily in the body. Thus also, according to Plato, Providence is deity, but Fate is something divine, and not a god: for it depends upon Providence, of which it is, as it were, the image. As Providence too is to intelligibles, so is Fate to sensibles. And alternately as Providence is to Fate, so are intelligibles to sensibles. But intelligibles are the first of beings, and from these others derive their subsistence. And hence the order of Fate depends on the dominion of Providence.

In the second place, let us look to the rational nature itself, when correcting the inaccuracy of sensible information, as when it accuses the sight of deception, in seeing the orb of the sun as not larger than a foot in diameter; when it represses the ebullitions of anger, and exclaims with Ulysses,

"Endure my heart;"

or when it restrains the wanton tendencies of desire to corporeal delight. For in all such operations it manifestly subdues the irrational motions, both gnostic and appetitive, and absolves itself from them, as from things foreign to its nature. But it is necessary to investigate the essence of every thing, not from its perversion, but from its energies according to nature. If therefore reason, when it energizes in us as reason, restrains the shadowy impression of the delights of licentious desire, punishes the precipitate motion of fury, and reproves the senses as full of deception, asserting that

"We nothing accurate, or see, or hear:"[34]

and if it says this, looking to its internal reasons, none of which it knows through the body, or through corporeal cognitions, it is evident that, according to this energy, it removes itself far from the senses, contrary to the decision of which it becomes separated from those sorrows and delights.

After this, let us direct our attention to another and a better motion of our rational soul, when, during the tranquillity of the inferior parts, by a self-convertive energy, it sees its own essence, the powers which it contains, the harmonic reasons from which it consists, and the many lives of which it is the middle boundary, and thus finds itself to be a rational world, the image of prior natures from which it proceeds, but the paradigm of such as are posterior to itself. To this energy of the soul, theoretic arithmetic and geometry greatly contribute; for these remove it from the senses, purify the intellect from the irrational forms of life with which it is surrounded, and lead it to the incorporeal perception of ideas. For if these sciences receive the soul replete with images, and knowing nothing subtle, and unattended with material garrulity; and if they elucidate reasons possessing an irrefragable necessity of demonstration, and forms full of all certainty and immateriality, and which by no means call to their aid the inaccuracy of sensibles, do they not evidently purify our intellectual life from things which fill us with a privation of intellect, and which impede our perception of true being?

After both these operations of the rational soul, let us now survey her highest intelligence, through which she sees her sister souls in the universe, who are allotted a residence in the heavens, and in the whole of a visible nature, according to the will of the fabricator of the world. But above all souls she sees intellectual essences and orders. For a deiform intellect resides above every soul, and which also imparts to the soul an intellectual habit. Prior to these, however, she sees those divine monads, from which all intellectual multitudes receive their unions. For above all things united, there must necessarily be unific causes; above things vivified, vivifying causes; above intellectual natures, those that impart intellect; and above all participants, imparticipable natures. From all these elevating modes of intelligence, it must be obvious to such as are not perfectly blind, how the soul, leaving sense and body behind, surveys through the projecting energies of intellect those beings that are entirely exempt from all connection with a corporeal nature.

The rational and intellectual soul therefore, in whatever manner it may be moved according to nature, is beyond body and sense. And hence it must necessarily have an essence separate from both. But from this again, it becomes manifest, that when it energizes according to its nature, it is superior to Fate, and beyond the reach of its attractive power; but that, when falling into sense and things irrational and corporalized, it follows downward natures, and lives with them as with inebriated neighbours, then together with them it becomes subject to the dominion of Fate. For again, it is necessary that there should be an order of beings of such a kind, as to subsist according to essence above Fate, but to be sometimes ranked under it according to habitude. For if there are beings, and such are all intellectual natures, which are eternally established above the laws of Fate, and also such which, according to the whole of their life, are distributed under the periods of Fate, it is necessary that the medium between these should be that nature which is sometimes above, and sometimes under the dominion of Fate. For the procession of incorporeal natures is much more without a vacuum than that of bodies.

The free will therefore of man, according to Plato, is a rational elective power, desiderative of true and apparent good, and leading the soul to both, through which it ascends and descends, errs and acts with rectitude. And hence the elective will be the same with that which characterizes our essence. According to this power, we differ from divine and mortal natures: for each of these is void of that two-fold inclination; the one on account of its excellence being alone established in true good; but the other in apparent good, on account of its defect. Intellect too characterizes the one, but sense the other; and the former, as Plotinus says, is our king, but the latter our messenger. We therefore are established in the elective power as a medium; and having the ability of tending both to true and apparent good, when we tend to the former we follow the guidance of intellect, when to the latter, that of sense. The power therefore which is in us is not capable of all things. For the power which is omnipotent is characterized by unity; and on this account is all-powerful, because it is one, and possesses the form of good. But the elective power is two-fold, and on this account is not able to effect all things; because by its inclinations to true and apparent good, it falls short of that nature which is prior to all things. It would however be all-powerful, if it had not an elective impulse, and was will alone. For a life subsisting according to will alone subsists according to good, because the will naturally tends to good, and such a life makes that which is characteristic in us most powerful and deiform. And hence through this the soul, according to Plato, becomes divine, and in another life, in conjunction with deity, governs the world. And thus much for the outlines of the leading dogmas of the philosophy of Plato.

In the beginning of this Introduction, I observed that, in drawing these outlines, I should conduct the reader through novel and solitary paths;—solitary indeed they must be since they have been unfrequented from the reign of the emperor Justinian to the present time; and novel they will doubtless appear to readers of every description, and particularly to those who have been nursed as it were in the bosom of matter, the pupils of experiment, the darlings of sense, and the legitimate descendants of the earth-born race that warred on the Olympian gods. To such as these, who have gazed on the dark and deformed face of their nurse, till they are incapable of beholding the light of truth, and who are become so drowsy from drinking immoderately of the cup of oblivion, that their whole life is nothing more than a transmigration from sleep to sleep, and from dream to dream, like men passing from one bed to another,—to such as these, the road through which we have been travelling will appear to be a delusive passage, and the objects which we have surveyed to be nothing more than phantastic visions, seen only by the eye of imagination, and when seen, idle and vain as the dreams of a shadow.

The following arguments, however, may perhaps awaken some few of these who are less lethargic than the rest, from the sleep of sense, and enable them to elevate their mental eye from the dark mire in which they are plunged, and gain a glimpse of this most weighty truth, that there is another world, of which this is nothing more than a most obscure resemblance, and another life, of which this is but the flying mockery. My present discourse therefore is addressed to those who consider experiment as the only solid criterion of truth.

In the first place then, these men appear to be ignorant of the invariable laws of demonstration properly so called, and that the necessary requisites of all demonstrative propositions[35] are these: that they exist as causes, are primary, more excellent, peculiar, true, and known than the conclusions. For every demonstration not only consists of principles prior to others, but of such as are eminently first; since if the assumed propositions may be demonstrated by other assumptions, such propositions may indeed appear prior to the conclusions, but are by no means entitled to the appellation of first. Others, on the contrary, which require no demonstration, but are of themselves manifest, are deservedly esteemed the first, the truest, and the best. Such indemonstrable truths were called by the ancients axioms from their majesty and authority, as the assumptions which constitute demonstrative syllogisms derive all their force and efficacy from these.

In the next place, they seem not to be sufficiently aware, that universal is better than partial demonstration. For *that* demonstration is the more excellent which is derived from the better cause; but a universal is more extended and excellent than a partial cause; since the arduous investigation of *the why* in any subject is only stopped by the arrival at universals. Thus if we desire to know why the outward angles of a triangle are equal to four right angles, and it is answered, Because the triangle is isosceles; we again ask, But why because isosceles? And if it be replied, Because it is a triangle; we may again inquire, But why because a triangle? To which we finally answer, because a triangle is a right-lined figure. And here our inquiry rests at that universal idea, which embraces every preceding particular one, and is contained in no other more general and comprehensive than itself. Add too, that the demonstration of particulars is almost the demonstration of infinites; of universals the demonstration of finites; and of infinites there can be no science. *That* demonstration likewise is the best which furnishes the mind with the most ample knowledge; and this is alone the province of universals. We may also add, that he who knows universals knows particulars likewise in capacity; but we cannot infer that he who has the best knowledge of particulars knows any thing of universals. And lastly, that which is universal is the object of intellect and reason; but particulars are coordinated to the perceptions of sense.

But here perhaps the experimentalist will say, admitting all this to be true, yet we no otherwise obtain a perception of these universals than by an induction of particulars, and abstraction from sensibles. To this I answer that the universal which is the proper object of science, is not by any means the offspring of abstraction; and induction is no otherwise subservient to its existence than as an exciting cause. For if scientific conclusions are indubitable, if the truth of demonstration is necessary and eternal, this universal is *truly all*, and not like that gained by abstraction, limited to a certain number of particulars. Thus the proposition that the angles of *every* triangle are equal to two right, if it is indubitably true, that is, if the term *every* in it *really* includes *all* triangles, cannot be the result of any abstraction; for this, however extended it may be, is limited, and falls far short of *universal* comprehension. Whence is it then that the dianoëtic power concludes thus confidently that the proposition is true of *all* triangles? For if it be said that the mind, after having abstracted triangle from a certain number of particulars, adds from itself what is wanting to complete the *all;* in the first place, no man, I believe, will say that any such operation as this took place in his mind when he first learnt this proposition; and in the next place, if this should be granted, it would follow that such proposition is a mere fiction, since it is uncertain whether that which is added to complete the *all* is *truly* added; and thus the conclusion will no longer be *indubitably necessary*.

In short, if the words *all* and *every*, with which every page of theoretic mathematics is full, mean what they are conceived by all men to mean, and if the universals which they signify are the proper objects of science, such universals must subsist in the soul prior to the energies of sense. Hence it will follow that induction is no otherwise subservient to science, than as it produces credibility in axioms and petitions; and this by exciting the universal conception of these latent in the soul. The particulars, therefore, of which an induction is made in order to produce science, must be so simple, that they may be immediately apprehended, and that the universal may be predicated of them without hesitation. The particulars of the experimentalists are not of this kind, and therefore never can be sources of science truly so called.

Of this, however, the man of experiment appears to be totally ignorant, and in consequence of this, he is likewise ignorant that parts can only be truly known through wholes, and that this is particularly the case with parts when they belong to a whole, which, as we have already observed, from comprehending in itself the parts which it produces, is called a whole prior to parts. As he, therefore, would by no means merit the appellation of a physician who should attempt to cure any part of the human body without a previous knowledge of the whole; so neither can he know any thing truly of the vegetable life of plants, who has not a previous knowledge of that vegetable life which subsists in the earth as a whole prior to, because the principle and cause of, all partial vegetable life, and who still prior to this has not a knowledge of that greater whole of this kind which subsists in nature herself; nor, as Hippocrates justly observes, can he know any thing truly of the nature of the human body who is ignorant what nature is considered as a great comprehending whole. And if this be true, and it is so most indubitably, with all physiological inquiries, how much more must it be the case with respect to a knowledge of those incorporeal forms to which we ascended in the first part of this Introduction, and which in consequence of proceeding from wholes entirely exempt from body are participated by it, with much greater obscurity and imperfection? Here then is the great difference, and a mighty one it is, between the knowledge gained by the most elaborate experiments, and that acquired by scientific reasoning, founded on the spontaneous, unperverted, and self-luminous conceptions of the soul. The former does not even lead its votary up to that one nature of the earth from which the natures of all the animals and plants on its surface, and of all the minerals and metals in its interior parts, blossom as from a perennial root. The latter conducts its votary through all the several mundane wholes up to that great whole the world itself, and thence leads him through the luminous order of incorporeal wholes to that vast whole of wholes, in which all other wholes are centred and rooted, and which is no other than the principle of all principles, and the fountain of deity itself. No less remarkable likewise is the difference between the tendencies of the two pursuits: for the one elevates the soul to the most luminous heights, and to that great ineffable which is beyond all altitude; but the other is the cause of a mighty calamity to the soul, since, according to the elegant expression of Plutarch, it extinguishes her principal and brightest eye, the knowledge of divinity. In short, the one leads to all that is grand, sublime and splendid in the universe; the other to all that is little, grovelling[36] and dark. The one is the parent of the most pure and ardent piety; the genuine progeny of the other are impiety and atheism. And, in fine, the one confers on its votary the most sincere, permanent, and exalted delight; the other continual disappointment, and unceasing molestation.

If such then are the consequences, such the tendencies of experimental inquiries, when prosecuted as the criterion of truth, and daily experience[37] unhappily shows that they are, there can be no other remedy for this enormous evil than the intellectual philosophy of Plato. So obviously excellent indeed is the tendency of this philosophy, that its author, for a period of more than two thousand years, has been universally celebrated by the epithet of divine. Such too is its preeminence, that it may be shown, without much difficulty, that the greatest men of antiquity, from the time in which its salutary light first blessed the human race, have been more or less imbued with its sacred principles, have been more or less the votaries of its divine truths. Thus, to mention a few from among a countless multitude. In the catalogue of those endued with sovereign power, it had for its votaries Dion the Siracusian, Julian the Roman, and Chosroes the Persian, emperor; among the leaders of armies, it had Chabrias and Phocion, those brave generals of the Athenians; among mathematicians, those leading stars of science, Eudoxus, Archimedes[38] and Euclid; among biographers, the inimitable Plutarch; among physicians, the admirable Galen; among rhetoricians, those unrivalled orators Demosthenes and Cicero; among critics, that prince of philologists, Longinus; and among poets, the most learned and majestic Virgil. Instances, though not equally illustrious, yet approximating to these in splendour, may doubtless be adduced after the fall of the Roman empire; but then they have been formed on these great ancients as models, and are, consequently, only rivulets from Platonic streams. And instances of excellence in philosophic attainments, similar to those among the Greeks, might have been enumerated among the moderns, if the hand of barbaric despotism had not compelled philosophy to retire into the deepest solitude, by demolishing her schools, and involving the human intellect in Cimmerian darkness. In our own country, however, though no one appears to have wholly devoted himself to the study of this philosophy, and he who does not will never penetrate its depths, yet we have a few bright examples of no common proficiency in its more accessible parts. The instances I allude to are Shaftesbury, Akenside, Harris, Petwin, and Sydenham. So splendid is the specimen of philosophic abilities displayed by these writers, like the fair dawning of some unclouded morning, that we have only deeply to regret that the sun of their genius set, before we were gladdened with its effulgence. Had it shone with its full strength, the writer of this Introduction would not have attempted either to translate the works, or elucidate the doctrines of Plato; but though it rose with vigour, it dispersed not the clouds in which its light was gradually involved, and the eye in vain anxiously waited for its meridian beam.

In short, the principles of the philosophy of Plato are of all others the most friendly to true piety, pure morality, solid learning, and sound government. For as it is scientific in all its parts, and in these parts comprehends all that can be known by man in theology and ethics, and all that is necessary for him to know in physics, it must consequently contain in itself the source of all that is great and good both to individuals and communities, must necessarily exalt while it benefits, and deify while it exalts.

We have said that this philosophy at first shone forth through Plato with an occult and venerable splendour; and it is owing to the hidden manner in which it is delivered by him, that its depth was not fathomed till many ages after its promulgation, and when fathomed, was treated by superficial readers with ridicule and contempt. Plato indeed is not singular in delivering his philosophy occultly: for this was the custom of all the great ancients; a custom not originating from a wish to become tyrants in knowledge, and keep the multitude in ignorance, but from a profound conviction that the sublimest truths are profaned when clearly unfolded to the vulgar. This indeed must necessarily follow; since, as Socrates in Plato justly observes, "it is not lawful for the pure to be touched by the impure;" and the multitude are neither purified from the defilements of vice, nor the darkness of two-fold ignorance. Hence, while they are thus doubly impure, it is as impossible for them to perceive the splendours of truth, as for an eye buried in mire to survey the light of day.

The depth of this philosophy then does not appear to have been perfectly penetrated except by the immediate disciples of Plato, for more than five hundred years after its first propagation. For though Crantor, Atticus, Albinus, Galen, and Plutarch, were men of great genius, and made no common proficiency in philosophic attainments, yet they appear not to have developed the profundity of Plato's conceptions; they withdrew not the veil which covers his secret meaning, like the curtains[39] which guarded the adytum of temples from the profane eye; and they saw not that all behind the veil is luminous, and that there divine spectacles[40] every where present themselves to the view. This task was reserved for men who were born indeed in a baser age, but who being allotted a nature similar to their leader, were the true interpreters of his mystic speculations. The most conspicuous of these are, the great Plotinus, the most learned Porphyry, the divine Iamblichus, the most acute Syrianus, Proclus the consummation of philosophic excellence, the magnificent Hierocles, the concisely elegant Sallust, and the most inquisitive Damascius. By

these men, who were truly links of the golden chain of deity, all that
is sublime, all that is mystic in the doctrines of Plato (and they are
replete with both these in a transcendent degree), was freed from its
obscurity and unfolded into the most pleasing and admirable light.
Their labours, however, have been ungratefully received. The
beautiful light which they benevolently disclosed has hitherto
unnoticed illumined philosophy in her desolate retreats, like a lamp
shining on some venerable statue amidst dark and solitary ruins. The
prediction of the master has been unhappily fulfilled in these his most
excellent disciples.

> "For an attempt of this kind," says he,[41] "will only be beneficial
> to a few, who from small vestiges, previously demonstrated, are
> themselves able to discover these abstruse particulars. But with
> respect to the rest of mankind, some it will fill with a contempt
> by no means elegant, and others with a lofty and arrogant hope,
> that they shall now learn certain excellent things."

Thus with respect to these admirable men, the last and the most
legitimate of the followers of Plato, some from being entirely
ignorant of the abstruse dogmas of Plato, and finding these
interpreters full of conceptions which are by no means obvious to
every one in the writings of that philosopher, have immediately
concluded that such conceptions are mere jargon and revery, that they
are not truly Platonic, and that they are nothing more than streams
which, though originally derived from a pure fountain, have become
polluted by distance from their source. Others, who pay attention to
nothing but the most exquisite purity of language, look down with
contempt upon every writer who lived after the fall of the
Macedonian empire; as if dignity and weight of sentiment were
inseparable from splendid and accurate diction; or as if it were
impossible for elegant writers to exist in a degenerate age. So far is this
from being the case, that though the style of Plotinus[42] and
Iamblichus[43] is by no means to be compared with that of Plato, yet
this inferiority is lost in the depth and sublimity of their conceptions,
and is as little regarded by the intelligent reader, as motes in a sun-
beam by the eye that gladly turns itself to the solar light.

As to the style of Porphyry, when we consider that he was the disciple of Longinus, whom Eunapius elegantly calls "a certain living library, and walking museum,"[44] it is but reasonable to suppose that he imbibed some portion of his master's excellence in writing. That he did so is abundantly evident from the testimony of Eunapius, who particularly commends his style, for its *clearness, purity,* and *grace.* "Hence," says he, "Porphyry being let down to men like a mercurial chain, through his various erudition, unfolded every thing into perspicuity and purity."[45] And in another place he speaks of him as abounding with all the graces of diction, and as the only one that exhibited and proclaimed the praise of his master.[46] With respect to the style of Proclus, it is pure, clear and elegant, like that of Dionysius Halicarnassus, but is much more copious and magnificent; that of Hierocles is venerable and majestic, and nearly equals the style of the greatest ancients; that of Sallust possesses an accuracy and a pregnant brevity, which cannot easily be distinguished from the composition of the Stagirite; and lastly, that of Damascius is clear and accurate, and highly worthy a most investigating mind.

Others again have filled themselves with a vain confidence, from reading the commentaries of these admirable interpreters, and have in a short time considered themselves superior to their masters. This was the case with Ficinus, Picus, Dr. Henry Moore, and other pseudo Platonists, their contemporaries, who, in order to combine Christianity with the doctrines of Plato, rejected some of his most important tenets, and perverted others, and thus corrupted one of these systems, and afforded no real benefit to the other.

But who are the men by whom these latter interpreters of Plato are reviled? When and whence did this defamation originate? Was it when the fierce champions for the trinity fled from Galilee to the groves of Academus, and invoked, but in vain, the assistance of Philosophy? When

> The trembling grove confess'd its fright,
> The wood-nymphs started at the sight;
> Ilissus backward urg'd his course,
> And rush'd indignant to his source.

Was it because that mitered sophist, Warburton, thought fit to talk of the polluted streams of the Alexandrian school, without knowing any

thing of the source whence those streams are derived? Or was it
because some heavy German critic, who knew nothing beyond a verb
in μι, presumed to *grunt*[47] at these venerable heroes? Whatever was its
source, and whenever it originated, for I have not been able to
discover either, this however is certain, that it owes its being to the
most profound Ignorance, or the most artful Sophistry, and that its
origin is no less contemptible than obscure. For let us but for a
moment consider the advantages which these latter Platonists
possessed beyond any of their modern revilers. In the first place, they
had the felicity of having the Greek for their native language, and
must therefore, as they were confessedly learned men, have
understood that language incomparably better than any man since
the time in which the ancient Greek was a living tongue. In the next
place, they had books to consult, written by the immediate disciples
of Plato, which have been lost for upwards of a thousand years, besides
many Pythagoric writings from which Plato himself derived most of
his more sublime dogmas. Hence we find the works of Parmenides,
Empedocles, the Eleatic Zeno, Speusippus, Xenocrates, and many
other illustrious philosophers of the highest antiquity, who were
either genuine Platonists, or the sources of Platonism, are continually
cited by these most excellent interpreters. And in the third place they
united the greatest abilities to the most unwearied exertions, the
greatest purity of life to the most piercing vigour of intellect. Now
when it is considered that the philosophy to the study of which these
great men devoted their lives, was professedly delivered by its author
in obscurity; that Aristotle himself studied it for twenty years; and
that it was no uncommon thing, as Plato informs us in one of his
Epistles, to find students unable to comprehend its sublimest tenets
even in a longer period than this,—when all these circumstances are
considered, what must we think of the arrogance, not to say
impudence, of men in the seventeenth, eighteenth, and nineteenth
centuries, who have dared to calumniate these great masters of
wisdom? Of men, with whom the Greek is no native language; who
have no such books to consult as those had whom they revile; who
have never thought, even in a dream, of making the acquisition of
wisdom the great object of their life; and who in short have
committed that most baneful error of mistaking philology

philosophy, and words for things? When such as these dare to defame men who may be justly ranked among the greatest and wisest of the ancients, what else can be said, than that they are the legitimate descendants of the suitors of Penelope, whom, in the animated language of Ulysses,

> Laws or divine or human fail'd to move,
> Or shame of men, or dread of gods above:
> Heedless alike of infamy or praise,
> Or Fame's eternal voice in future days.[48]

But it is now time to present the reader with a general view of the works of Plato, and also to speak of the preambles, digressions, and style of their author, and of the following translation.* In accomplishing the first of these, I shall avail myself of the Synopsis of Mr. Sydenham, taking the liberty at the same time of correcting it where it appears to be erroneous, and of making additions to it where it appears to be deficient.

The dialogues of Plato are of various kinds; not only with regard to those different matters, which are the subjects of them; but in respect of the manner also, in which they are composed or framed, and of the form under which they make their appearance to the reader. It will therefore, as I imagine, be not improper, in pursuance of the admonition given us by Plato himself in his dialogue named *Phædrus*,[49] and in imitation of the example set us by the ancient Platonists,[50] to distinguish the several kinds; by dividing them, first, into the most general; and then, subdividing into the subordinate; till we come to those lower species, that particularly and precisely denote the nature of the several dialogues, and from which they ought to take their respective denominations.

The most general division of the writings of Plato, is into those of the Sceptical kind, and those of the Dogmatical. In the former sort, nothing is expressly either proved or asserted: some philosophical question only is considered and examined; and the reader is left to himself to draw such conclusions, and discover such truths, as the philosopher means to insinuate. This is done, either in the way of

---

* This and other similar references refer to Taylor's five volume set of the complete *Works of Plato*, originally published in 1804.

inquiry, or in the way of controversy and dispute. In the way of controversy are carried on all such dialogues, as tend to eradicate false opinions; and that, either indirectly, by involving them in difficulties, and embarrassing the maintainers of them; or directly, by confuting them. In the way of inquiry proceed those, whose tendency is to raise in the mind right opinions; and that, either by exciting to the pursuit of some part of wisdom, and showing in what manner to investigate it; or by leading the way, and helping the mind forward in the search. And this is effected by a process through opposing arguments.[51]

The dialogues of the other kind, the Dogmatical or Didactic, teach explicitly some point of doctrine: and this they do, either by laying it down in the authoritative way, or by proving it in the way of reason and argument. In the authoritative way the doctrine is delivered, sometimes by the speaker himself magisterially, at other times as derived to him by tradition from wise men. The argumentative or demonstrative method of teaching, used by Plato, proceeds in all the dialectic ways, *dividing, defining, demonstrating,* and *analyzing;* and the object of it consists in exploring truth alone.

According to this division is framed the following scheme, or table:

DIALOGUES[52]			
SCEPTICAL	DISPUTATIVE	EMBARRASSING	
		CONFUTING	
	INQUISITIVE	EXCITING	
		ASSISTING	
DOGMATICAL	DEMONSTRATIVE	ANALYTICAL	
		INDUCTIONAL	
	AUTHORITATIVE	MAGISTERIAL	
		TRADITIONAL	

The philosopher, in thus varying his manner, and diversifying his writings into these several kinds, means not merely to entertain with their variety; nor to teach, on different occasions, with more or less plainness and perspicuity; nor yet to insinuate different degrees of certainty in the doctrines themselves: but he takes this method, as a consummate master of the art of composition in the dialogue-way of writing, from the different characters of the speakers, as from different elements in the frame of these dramatic dialogues, or different ingredients in their mixture, producing some peculiar genius, and turn of temper, as it were, in each.

Socrates indeed is in almost all of them the principal speaker: but when he falls into the company of some arrogant sophist; when the modest wisdom, and clear science of the one, are contrasted with the confident ignorance, and blind opinionativeness of the other; dispute and controversy must of course arise: where the false pretender cannot fail of being either puzzled or confuted. To puzzle him only is sufficient, if there be no other persons present; because such a man can never be confuted in his own opinion: but when there is an audience round them, in danger of being misled by sophistry into error, then is the true philosopher to exert his utmost, and the vain sophist to be convicted and exposed.

In some dialogues Plato represents his great master mixing in conversation with young men of the best families in the common-wealth. When these happen to have docile dispositions and fair minds, then is occasion given to the philosopher to call forth[53] the latent seeds of wisdom, and to cultivate the noble plants with true doctrine, in the affable and familiar way of joint inquiry. To this is owing the inquisitive genius of such dialogues: where, by a seeming equality in the conversation, the curiosity or zeal of the mere stranger is excited; that of the disciple is encouraged; and by proper questions, the mind is aided and forwarded in the search of truth.

At other times, the philosophic hero of these dialogues is introduced in a higher character, engaged in discourse with men of more improved understandings and enlightened minds. At such seasons he has an opportunity of teaching in a more explicit manner, and of discovering the reasons of things: for to such an audience truth is due, and all demonstration[54] possible in the teaching it. Hence, in the dialogues composed of these persons, naturally arises the justly argumentative or demonstrative genius; and this, as we have before observed, according to all the dialectic methods.

But when the doctrine to be taught admits not of demonstration;

of which kind is the doctrine of antiquities, being only traditional, and a matter of belief; and the doctrine of laws, being injunctional, and the matter of obedience; the air of authority is then assumed: in the former cases, the doctrine is traditionally handed down to others from the authority of ancient sages; in the latter, is magisterially pronounced with the authority of a legislator.[55]

Thus much for the manner, in which the dialogues of Plato are severally composed, and the cast of genius given them in their composition. The form under which they appear, or the external character that marks them, is of three sorts; either purely dramatic, like the dialogue of tragedy or comedy; or purely narrative, where a former conversation is supposed to be committed to writing, and communicated to some absent friend; or of the mixed kind, like a narration in dramatic poems, where is recited, to some person present, the story of things past.

Having thus divided the dialogues of Plato, in respect of that inward form or composition, which creates their genius; and again, with reference to that outward form, which marks them, like flowers and other vegetables, with a certain character; we are further to make a division of them, with regard to their subject and their design; beginning with their design, or end, because for the sake of this are all the subjects chosen. The end of all the writings of Plato is that which is the end of all true philosophy or wisdom, the perfection and the happiness of man. Man therefore is the general subject; and the first business of philosophy must be to inquire, what is that being called man, who is to be made happy; and what is his nature, in the perfection of which is placed his happiness. As however, in the preceding part of this Introduction, we have endeavoured to give the outlines of Plato's doctrine concerning man, it is unnecessary in this place to say any thing further on that subject.

The dialogues of Plato, therefore, with respect to their subjects, may be divided into the speculative, the practical, and such as are of a mixed nature. The subjects of these last are either general, comprehending both the others; or differential, distinguishing them. The general subjects are either fundamental, or final: those of the fundamental kind are philosophy, human nature, the soul of man; of the final kind are love, beauty, good. The differential regard knowledge, as it stands related to practice; in which are considered two questions: one of which is, whether virtue is to be taught; the other is, whether error in the will depends on error in the judgment. The subjects of the speculative dialogues relate either to words, or to things. Of the former sort are etymology, sophistry, rhetoric, poetry: of the latter sort are science, true being, the principles of mind, outward nature. The practical subjects relate either to private conduct, and the government of the mind over the whole man; or to his duty towards others in his several relations; or to the government of a civil state, and the public conduct of a whole people. Under these three heads rank in order the particular subjects practical; virtue in general, sanctity, temperance, fortitude; justice, friendship, patriotism, piety; the ruling mind in a civil government, the frame and order of a state, law in general, and lastly, those rules of government and of public conduct, the civil laws.

Thus, for the sake of giving the reader a scientific, that is, a comprehensive, and at the same time a distinct, view of Plato's writings, we have attempted to exhibit to him their just and natural distinctions; whether he chooses to consider them with regard to their inward form or essence, their outward form or appearance, their matter, or their end: that is, in those more familiar terms, we have used in this Synopsis, their genius, their character, their subject, and their design.

And here it is requisite to observe, that as it is the characteristic of the highest good to be universally beneficial, though some things are benefitted by it more and others less, in consequence of their greater or less aptitude to receive it; in like manner the dialogues of Plato are so largely stamped with the characters of sovereign good, that they are calculated to benefit in a certain degree even those who are incapable of penetrating their profundity. They can tame a savage sophist, like Thrasymachus in the Republic; humble the arrogance even of those who are ignorant of their ignorance; make those to become proficients in political, who will never arrive at theoretic virtue; and, in short, like the illuminations of deity, wherever there is any portion of aptitude in their recipients, they purify, irradiate, and exalt.

After this general view of the dialogues of Plato, let us in the next place consider their preambles, the digressions with which they abound, and the character of the style in which they are written. With respect to the first of these, the preambles, however superfluous they may at first sight appear, they will be found on a closer inspection necessary to the design of the dialogues which they accompany. Thus the prefatory part of the Timæus unfolds, in images agreeably to the Pythagoric custom, the theory of the world; and the first part of the Parmenides, or the discussion of ideas, is in fact merely a preamble to the second part, or the speculation of *the one;* to which however it is essentially preparatory. Hence, as Plutarch says, when he speaks of Plato's dialogue on the Atlantic island: These preambles are superb gates and magnificent courts with which he purposely embellishes his great edifices, that nothing may be wanting to their beauty, and that all may be equally splendid. He acts, as Dacier well observes, like a great prince, who, when he builds a sumptuous palace, adorns (in the language of Pindar) the vestibule with golden pillars. For it is fit that what is first seen should be splendid and magnificent, and should as it were perspicuously announce all that grandeur which afterwards presents itself to the view.

With respect to the frequent digressions in his dialogues, these also, when accurately examined, will be found to be no less subservient to the leading design of the dialogues in which they are introduced; at the same time that they afford a pleasing relaxation to the mind from the labour of severe investigation. Hence Plato, by the most happy and enchanting art, contrives to lead the reader to the temple of Truth, through the delightful groves and valleys of the Graces. In short, this circuitous course, when attentively considered, will be found to be the shortest road by which he could conduct the reader to the desired end: for in accomplishing this it is necessary to regard not that road which is most straight in the nature of things, or abstractedly considered, but that which is most direct in the progressions of human understanding.

With respect to the style of Plato, though it forms in reality the most inconsiderable part of the merit of his writings, style in all philosophical works being the last thing that should be attended to, yet even in this Plato may contend for the palm of excellence with the most renowned masters of diction. Hence we find that his style was the admiration of the finest writers of antiquity. According to Ammianus,

Jupiter himself would not speak otherwise, if he were to converse in the Attic tongue. Aristotle considered his style as a medium between poetry and prose. Cicero no less praises him for the excellence of his diction than the profundity of his conceptions; and Longinus calls him, with respect to his language, the rival of Homer. Hence he is considered by this prince of critics, as deriving into himself abundant streams from the Homeric fountain, and is compared by him, in his rivalship of Homer, to a new antagonist, who enters the lists against one that is already the object of universal admiration.

Notwithstanding this praise, however, Plato has been accused, as Longinus informs us, of being frequently hurried away as by a certain Bacchic fury of words to immoderate and unpleasant metaphors, and an allegoric magnificence of diction.[56] Longinus excuses this by saying, that whatever naturally excels in magnitude possesses very little of purity. For that, says he, which is in every respect accurate is in danger of littleness. He adds:

> "and may not this also be necessary, that those of an abject and moderate genius, because they never encounter danger, nor aspire after the summit of excellence, are for the most part without error and remain in security; but that great things become insecure through their magnitude?"

Indeed it appears to me, that whenever this exuberance, this Bacchic fury, occurs in the diction of Plato, it is owing to the magnitude of the inspiring influence of deity with which he is then replete. For that he sometimes wrote from divine inspiration is evident from his own confession in the Phædrus, a great part of which is not so much like an orderly discourse as a dithyrambic poem. Such a style therefore, as it is the progeny of divine mania, which, as Plato justly observes, is better than all human prudence, spontaneously adapts itself to its producing cause, imitates a supernatural power as far as this can be effected by words, and thus necessarily becomes magnificent, vehement, and exuberant; for such are the characteristics of its source. All judges of composition however, both ancient and modern, are agreed that his style is in general graceful and pure; and that it is sublime without being impetuous and rapid. It is indeed no less harmonious than elevated, no less accurate[57] than magnificent. It combines the force of the greatest orators with the graces of the first of poets; and, in short, is a river to which those justly celebrated lines of Denham may be most pertinently applied:

Tho' deep, yet clear; tho' gentle, yet not dull;
Strong without rage, without o'erflowing full.

Having thus considered the philosophy of Plato, given a general view of his writings, and made some observations on his style, it only now remains to speak of my arrangement of his dialogues and translation of his works, and then, with a few appropriate observations, to close this Introduction.

As no accurate and scientific arrangement then of these dialogues has been transmitted to us from the ancients, I was under the necessity of adopting an arrangement of my own, which I trust is not unscientific, however inferior it may be to that which was doubtless made, though unfortunately lost, by the latter interpreters of Plato. In my arrangement, therefore, I have imitated the order of the universe, in which, as I have already observed, wholes precede parts, and universals particulars. Hence I have placed those dialogues first which rank as wholes, or have the relation of a system, and afterwards those in which these systems are branched out into particulars. Thus, after the First Alcibiades, which may be called, and appears to have been generally considered by the ancients, an introduction to the whole of Plato's philosophy, I have placed the Republic and the Laws, which may be said to comprehend systematically the morals and politics of Plato. After these I have ranked the Timæus, which contains the whole of his physiology, and together with it the Critias, because of its connection with the Timæus. The next in order is the Parmenides, which contains a system of his theology. Thus far this arrangement is conformable to the natural progress of the human mind in the acquisition of the sublimest knowledge: the subsequent arrangement principally regards the order of things. After the Parmenides then, the Sophista, Phædrus, Greater Hippias, and Banquet, follow, which may be considered as so many lesser wholes subordinate to and comprehended in the Parmenides, which, like the universe itself, is a whole of wholes. For in the Sophista *being itself* is investigated, in the Banquet *love itself*, and in the Phædrus *beauty itself;* all which are intelligible forms, and are consequently contained in the Parmenides, in which the whole extent of the intelligible is unfolded. The Greater Hippias is classed with the Phædrus, because in the latter the whole series of the beautiful is discussed, and in the former that which subsists in soul. After these follows the Theætetus, in which science considered as subsisting in soul is investigated; science itself, according to its first subsistence, having been previously celebrated by Socrates in one part of the Phædrus. The Politicus and Minos, which follow next, may be considered as ramifications from the Laws: and, in short, all the following dialogues either consider *more particularly* the dogmas which are *systematically* comprehended in those already enumerated, or naturally flow from them as their original source. As it did not however appear possible to arrange these dialogues which rank as parts in the same accurate order as those which we considered as wholes, it was thought better to class them either according to their agreement in one particular circumstance, as the Phædo, Apology, and Crito, all which relate to the death of Socrates, and as the Meno and Protagoras, which relate to the question whether virtue can be taught; or according to their agreement in character, as the Lesser Hippias and Euthydemus, which are *anatreptic*, and the Theages, Laches, and Lysis, which are *maieutic* dialogues. The Cratylus is ranked in the last place, not so much because the subject of it is etymology, as because a great part of it is deeply theological: for by this arrangement, after having ascended to all the divine orders and their ineffable principle in the Parmenides, and thence descended in a regular series to the human soul in the subsequent dialogues, the reader is again led back to deity in this dialogue, and thus imitates the order which all beings observe, that of incessantly returning to the principles whence they flow.

After the dialogues[58] follow the Epistles of Plato, which are in every respect worthy that prince of all true philosophers. They are not only written with great elegance, and occasionally with magnificence of diction, but with all the becoming dignity of a mind conscious of its superior endowments, and all the authority of a master in philosophy. They are likewise replete with many admirable political observations, and contain some of his most abstruse dogmas, which though delivered enigmatically, yet the manner in which they are delivered, elucidates at the same time that it is elucidated by what is said of these dogmas in his more theological dialogues.

With respect to the following translation,* it is necessary to observe, in the first place, that the number of the legitimate dialogues of Plato is fifty-five; for though the Republic forms but one treatise, and the Laws another, yet the former consists of ten and the latter of twelve books, and each of these books is a dialogue. Hence, as there are thirty-three dialogues, besides the Laws and the Republic, fifty-five will, as we have said, be the amount of the whole. Of these fifty-five, the nine following have been translated by Mr. Sydenham; *viz.* the First and Second Alcibiades, the Greater and Lesser Hippias, the Banquet (except the speech of Alcibiades), the Philebus, the Meno, the Io, and the Rivals.[59] I have already observed, and with deep regret, that this excellent though unfortunate scholar died before he had made that proficiency in the philosophy of Plato which might have been reasonably expected from so fair a beginning. I personally knew him only in the decline of life, when his mental powers were not only considerably impaired by age, but greatly injured by calamity. His life had been very stormy: his circumstances, for many years preceding his death, were indigent; his patrons were by no means liberal; and his real friends were neither numerous nor affluent. He began the study of Plato, as he himself informed me, when he had considerably passed the meridian of life, and with most unfortunate prejudices against his best disciples, which I attempted to remove during my acquaintance with him, and partly succeeded in the attempt; but infirmity and death prevented its completion. Under such circumstances it was not to be expected that he would fathom the profundity of Plato's conceptions, and arrive at the summit of philosophic attainments. I saw, however, that his talents and his natural disposition were such as might have ranked him among the best of Plato's interpreters, if he had not yielded to the pressure of calamity, if he had not nourished such baneful prejudices, and if he had not neglected philosophy in the early part of life. Had this happened, my labours would have been considerably lessened, or perhaps rendered entirely unnecessary, and

---

* This and other similar references refer to Taylor's five volume set of the complete *Works of Plato*, originally published in 1804.

his name would have been transmitted to posterity with undecaying renown. As this unfortunately did not happen, I have been under the necessity of diligently examining and comparing with the original all those parts of the dialogues which he translated, that are more deeply philosophical, or that contain any thing of the theology of Plato. In these, as might be expected, I found him greatly deficient; I found him sometimes mistaking the meaning through ignorance of Plato's more sublime tenets, and at other times perverting it, in order to favour some opinions of his own. His translation however of other parts which are not so abstruse is excellent. In these he not only presents the reader faithfully with the matter, but likewise with the genuine manner of Plato. The notes too which accompany the translation of these parts generally exhibit just criticism and extensive learning, an elegant taste, and a genius naturally philosophic. Of these notes I have preserved as much as was consistent with the limits and design of the following work.*

Of the translation of the Republic by Dr. Spens, it is necessary to observe, that a considerable part of it is very faithfully executed; but that in the more abstruse parts it is inaccurate; and that it every where abounds with Scotticisms which offend an English ear, and vulgarisms which are no less disgraceful to the translator than disgusting to the reader. Suffice it therefore to say of this version, that I have adopted it wherever I found it could with propriety be adopted, and given my own translation where it was otherwise.

Of the ten dialogues, translated by Dacier, I can say nothing with accuracy, because I have no knowledge whatever of the French language; but if any judgment may be formed of this work, from a translation of it into English, I will be bold to say that it is by no means literal, and that he very frequently mistakes the sense of the original. From this translation therefore I could derive but little assistance; some however I have derived, and that little I willingly acknowledge. In translating the rest of Plato's works, and this, as the reader may easily see, forms by far the greatest part of them, I have had no assistance from any translation except that of Ficinus, the

---

* This and other similar references refer to Taylor's five volume set of the complete *Works of Plato*, originally published in 1804.

general excellency of which is well known to every student of Plato, arising not only from his possessing a knowledge of Platonism superior to that of any translators that have followed him, but likewise from his having made this translation from a very valuable manuscript in the Medicean library, which is now no longer to be found. I have, however, availed myself of the learned labours of the editors of various dialogues of Plato; such as the edition of the Rivals, Euthyphro, Apology, Crito, and Phædo, by Forster; of the First and Second Alcibiades and Hipparchus, by Etwall; of the Meno, First Alcibiades, Phædo and Phædrus, printed at Vienna 1784; of the Cratylus and Theætetus, by Fischer; of the Republic, by Massey; and of the Euthydemus and Gorgias, by Dr. Routh, president of Magdalen College, Oxford. This last editor has enriched his edition of these two dialogues with very valuable and copious philological and critical notes, in which he has displayed no less learning than judgment, no less acuteness than taste. He appears indeed to me to be one of the best and most modest of philologists; and it is to be hoped that he will be imitated in what he has done by succeeding editors of Plato's text.

If my translation had been made with an eye to the judgment of the many, it would have been necessary to apologize for its literal exactness. Had I been anxious to gratify false taste with respect to composition, I should doubtless have attended less to the precise meaning of the original, have omitted almost all connective particles, have divided long periods into a number of short ones, and branched out the strong and deep river of Plato's language into smooth-gliding, shallow, and feeble streams; but as the present work was composed with the hope indeed of benefiting all, but with an eye to the criticism solely of men of elevated souls, I have endeavoured not to lose a word of the original; and yet at the same time have attempted to give the translation as much elegance as such verbal accuracy can be supposed capable of admitting. I have also endeavoured to preserve the manner as well as the matter of my author, being fully persuaded that no translation deserves applause, in which both these are not as much as possible preserved.

My principal object in this arduous undertaking* has been to

---

* *i.e.* his translation of the complete *Works of Plato.*

unfold all the abstruse and sublime dogmas of Plato, as they are found dispersed in his works. Minutely to unravel the art which he employs in the composition of all his dialogues, and to do full justice to his meaning in every particular, must be the task of some one who has more leisure, and who is able to give the works of Plato to the public on a more extensive plan. In accomplishing this great object, I have presented the reader in my notes with nearly the substance in English of all the following manuscript Greek Commentaries and Scholia on Plato; *viz.* of the Commentaries of Proclus on the Parmenides and First Alcibiades, and of his Scholia on the Cratylus; of the Scholia of Olympiodorus on the Phædo, Gorgias, and Philebus; and of Hermeas on the Phædrus. To these are added very copious extracts from the manuscript of Damascius,[60] Περι Αρχων, and from the published works of Proclus on the Timæus, Republic, and Theology of Plato. Of the four first of these manuscripts, three of which are folio volumes, I have complete copies taken with my own hand; and of the copious extracts from the others, those from Olympiodorus on the Gorgias were taken by me from the copy preserved in the British Museum: those from the same philosopher on the Philebus, and those from Hermeas on the Phædrus, and Damascius Περι Αρχων, from the copies in the Bodleian library.

And here gratitude demands that I should publicly acknowledge the very handsome and liberal manner in which I was received by the University of Oxford, and by the principal librarian, and sub-librarians of the Bodleian library, during the time that I made the above-mentioned extracts. In the first place I have to acknowledge the very polite attention which was paid to me by Dr. Jackson,[61] dean of Christchurch. In the second place, the liberty of attendance at the Bodleian library, and the accommodation which was there afforded me by the librarians, of that excellent collection, demand from me no small tribute of praise. And, above all, the very liberal manner in which I was received by the fellows of New College, with whom I resided for three weeks, and from whom I experienced even Grecian hospitality, will, I trust, be as difficult a task for time to obliterate from my memory, as it would be for me to express it as it deserves.[62]

With respect to the faults which I may have committed in my translation (for I am not vain enough to suppose it is without fault), I might plead as an excuse, that the whole of it has been executed amidst severe endurance from bodily infirmity and indigent circumstances; and that a very considerable part of it was accomplished amidst other ills of no common magnitude, and other labours inimical to such an undertaking. But whatever may be my errors, I will not fly to calamity for an apology. Let it be my excuse, that the mistakes I may have committed in lesser particulars, have arisen from my eagerness to seize and promulgate those great truths in the philosophy and theology of Plato, which though they have been concealed for ages in oblivion, have a subsistence coeval with the universe, and will again be restored, and flourish, for very extended periods, through all the infinite revolutions of time.

In the next place, it is necessary to speak concerning the qualifications requisite in a legitimate student of the philosophy of Plato, previous to which I shall just notice the absurdity of supposing, that a mere knowledge of the Greek tongue, however great that knowledge may be, is alone sufficient to the understanding the sublime doctrines of Plato; for a man might as well think that he can understand Archimedes without a knowledge of the elements of geometry, merely because he can read him in the original. Those who entertain such an idle opinion, would do well to meditate on the profound observation of Heraclitus, that "*polymathy does not teach intellect,*" (Πολυμαθιη νοον ου διδασκει).

By a legitimate student, then, of the Platonic philosophy, I mean one who, both from nature and education, is properly qualified for such an arduous undertaking: that is, one who possesses a naturally good disposition; is sagacious and acute, and is inflamed with an ardent desire for the acquisition of wisdom and truth; who from his childhood has been well instructed in the mathematical disciplines; who, besides this, has spent whole days, and frequently the greater part of the night, in profound meditation; and, like one triumphantly sailing over a raging sea, or skilfully piercing through an army of foes, has successfully encountered an hostile multitude of doubts;—in short, who has never considered *wisdom* as a thing of trifling estimation and easy access, but as that which cannot be obtained without the most generous and severe endurance, and the intrinsic worth of which surpasses all corporeal good, far more than the ocean the fleeting bubble which floats on its surface. To such as are destitute of these requisites, who make the study of words their sole employment, and the pursuit of wisdom but at best a secondary thing, who expect to be wise by desultory application for an hour or two in a day, after the fatigues of business, after mixing with the base multitude of mankind, laughing with the gay, affecting airs of gravity with the serious, tacitly assenting to every man's opinion, however absurd, and winking at folly however shameful and base—to such as these—and, alas! the world is full of such—the sublimest truths must appear to be nothing more than jargon and reverie, the dreams of a distempered imagination, or the ebullitions of fanatical faith.

But all this is by no means wonderful, if we consider that two-fold ignorance is the disease of *the many*. For they are not only ignorant with respect to the sublimest knowledge, but they are even ignorant of their ignorance. Hence they never suspect their want of understanding; but immediately reject a doctrine which appears at first sight absurd, because it is too splendid for their bat-like eyes to behold. Or if they even yield their assent to its truth, their very assent is the result of the same most dreadful disease of the soul. For they will fancy, says Plato, that they understand the highest truths, when the very contrary is really the case. I earnestly therefore entreat men of this description, not to meddle with any of the profound speculations of the Platonic philosophy; for it is more dangerous to urge them to such an employment, than to advise them to follow their sordid avocations with unwearied assiduity, and toil for wealth with increasing alacrity and vigour, as they will by this mean give free scope to the base habits of their soul, and sooner suffer that punishment which in such as these must always precede mental illumination, and be the inevitable consequence of guilt. It is well said indeed by Lysis,[63] the Pythagorean, that to inculcate liberal speculations and discourses to those whose morals are turbid and confused, is just as absurd as to pour pure and transparent water into a deep well full of mire and clay; for he who does this will only disturb the mud, and cause the pure water to become defiled. The woods of such, as the same author beautifully observes (that is the irrational or corporeal life), in which these dire passions are nourished, must first be purified with fire and sword, and every kind of instrument (that is through preparatory disciplines and the political virtues), and reason must be freed from its slavery to the affections, before any thing useful can be planted in these savage haunts.

Let not such then presume to explore the regions of Platonic philosophy. The land is too pure to admit the sordid and the base. The road which conducts to it is too intricate to be discovered by the unskilful and stupid, and the journey is too long and laborious to be accomplished by the effeminate and the timid, by the slave of passion and the dupe of opinion, by the lover of sense and the despiser of truth. The dangers and difficulties in the undertaking are such as can be sustained by none but the most hardy and accomplished adventurers; and he who begins the journey without the strength of Hercules, or the wisdom and patience of Ulysses, must be destroyed by the wild beasts of the forest, or perish in the storms of the ocean; must suffer transmutation into a beast, through the magic power of Circe, or be exiled for life by the detaining charms of Calypso; and in short must descend into Hades, and wander in its darkness, without emerging from thence to the bright regions of the morning, or be ruined by the deadly melody of the Siren's song. To the most skilful traveller, who pursues the right road with an ardour which no toils can abate, with a vigilance which no weariness can surprise into negligence, and with virtue which no temptations can seduce, it exhibits for many years the appearance of the Ithaca of Ulysses, or the flying Italy of Æneas; for we no sooner gain a glimpse of the pleasing land which is to be the end of our journey, than it is suddenly ravished from our view, and we still find ourselves at a distance from the beloved coast, exposed to the fury of a stormy sea of doubts.

Abandon then, ye grovelling souls, the fruitless design! Pursue with avidity the beaten road which leads to popular honours and sordid gain, but relinquish all thoughts of a voyage for which you are totally unprepared. Do you not perceive what a length of sea separates you from the royal coast? A sea,

> Huge, horrid, vast, where scarce in safety sails
> The best built ship, though Jove inspire the gales.

And may we not very justly ask you, similar to the interrogation of Calypso,

What ships have you, what sailors to convey,
What oars to cut the long laborious way?

I shall only observe further, that the life of Plato, by Olympiodorus, was prefixed to this translation,* in preference to that by Diogenes Laertius, because the former is the production of a most eminent Platonist, and the latter of a mere historian, who indiscriminately gave to the public whatever anecdotes he found in other authors. If the reader combines this short sketch of the life of Plato with what that philosopher says of himself in his 7th Epistle, he will be in possession of the most important particulars about him that can be obtained at present.

---

* This and other similar references refer to Taylor's five volume set of the complete *Works of Plato*, originally published in 1804.

Explanation of Certain Platonic Terms

Note: the following is a compilation of glossary terms given by Thomas Taylor in three of his principle works, as shown in the following key:

[Plato Works]	*The Works of Plato, viz. His Fifty-Five Dialogues and Twelve Epistles*, 1804, 5 vols.
[Procl. Theol. Plato.]	*The Six Books of Proclus on the Theology of Plato*, 1816, 2 vols.
[Procl. Comm. Timæus.]	*The Commentaries of Proclus on the Timæus of Plato* (2nd Edition), 1820, 2 vols.

As some apology may be thought necessary for having introduced, in the course of the following translation, certain unusual words of Greek origin, I shall only observe, that as all arts and sciences have certain appropriate terms peculiar to themselves, philosophy, which is the art of arts, and science of sciences, as being the mistress of both, has certainly a prior and a far superior claim to this privilege. I have not, however, introduced, I believe, any of these terms, without at the same time sufficiently explaining them; but, lest the contrary should have taken place, the following explanation of all such terms as I have been able to recollect, and also of common words used by Platonists in a peculiar sense, is subjoined for the information of the reader. [Plato Works]

TERMS

Alliation. Change in quality. [Procl. Comm. Timæus.]

Altermotive, the. That which is moved by another thing, and not by itself. [Procl. Comm. Timæus.]

Anagogic, αναγωγικος. Leading on high. [Plato Works]
Anagogic, the. That which elevates the soul from sensibles to intelligibles. [Procl. Comm. Timæus.]

Anger. (*thymos*) An appetite of the soul directed to the avengement of incidental molestations. [Procl. Comm. Timæus.]

Apocatastasis. Restitution to a pristine form, or condition of being. [Procl. Comm. Timæus.]

Composite, the, συνθετος. I have used the word composite instead of *compounded*, because the latter rather denotes the mingling than the contiguous union of one thing with another, which the former, through its derivation from the Latin word *compositus*, solely denotes. [Procl. Theol. Plato.] [Procl. Comm. Timæus.]

Demiurgus, δημιουργος. Jupiter, the artificer of the universe. [Plato Works]
Demiurgus of Wholes, δημιουργος των ολων. The artificer (maker) of the universe is thus denominated, because he produces the universe so far as it is a *whole*, and likewise all the *wholes* it contains, by his own immediate energy; other subordinate powers cooperating with him in the production of parts. Hence he produces the universe *totally* and *at once*. [Procl. Theol. Plato.] [Procl. Comm. Timæus.]

Desire, επιθυμια. Is an irrational appetite solely directed to external objects, and to the gratification arising from the possession of them. [Procl. Theol. Plato.]

Dianoia, διανοια, from whence *dianoëtic*, the discursive energy of reason; (διεξοδικη του λογου ενεργεια) or according to its most accurate signification, it is that power of the soul which reasons scientifically, deriving the principles of its reasoning from intellect, or the power which sees truth intuitively. [Procl. Theol. Plato.] [Procl. Comm. Timæus.]

Dianoetic. This word is derived from διανοια, or that power of the soul which reasons scientifically, deriving the principles of its reasoning from intellect. Plato is so uncommonly accurate in his diction, that this. word is very seldom used by him in any other than its primary sense. [Plato Works]

Divine, the,[1] το θειον, is *being* subsisting in conjunction with *the one*. For all things except *the one*, viz. essence, life and intellect, are considered by Plato as suspended from and secondary to the gods. For the gods do not subsist in, but prior to, these, which they also produce and connect, but are not characterized by these. In many places, however, Plato calls the participants of the gods by the names of the gods. For not only the Athenian guest in the Laws, but also Socrates in the Phædrus, calls a divine soul a god. "For," says he "all the horses and charioteers of *the gods* are good," etc. And afterwards, still more clearly, he adds, "And this is the life of *the gods*." And not only this, but he also denominates those natures gods, that are always united to the gods, and which, in conjunction with them, give completion to one series. He also frequently calls dæmons gods, though according to essence, they are secondary to, and subsist about, the gods. For in the Phædrus, Timæus, and other dialogues, he extends the appellation of the gods as far as to dæmons. And what is still more paradoxical than all this, he does not refuse to call some men gods; as, for instance, the Elean Guest in the Sophista. From all this, therefore, we must infer, that with respect to the word god, one thing which is thus denominated is simply deity; another is so according to union; a third, according to participation; a fourth, according to contact; and a fifth, according to similitude. Thus every superessential nature is primarily a god; but every intellectual nature is so according to union. And again, every divine soul is a god according to participation; but divine dæmons are gods, according to contact with the gods; and the souls of men obtain this appellation through similitude. Each of these, however, except the first, is, as we have said, rather divine than a god: for the Athenian Guest, in the Laws, calls intellect itself divine.

But that which is divine is secondary to the first deity, in the same manner as *the united* is to *the one; that which is intellectual*, to *intellect;* and *that which is animated*, to *soul.* Indeed, things more uniform and simple always precede; and the series of beings ends in *the one* itself. [Plato Works]

Doxastic. This word is derived from δόξα, *opinion*, and signifies that which is apprehended by opinion, or that power which is the extremity of the rational soul. This power knows the universal in particulars, as that *every* man is a rational animal; but it knows not the διοτι, or *why* a thing is, but only the οτι, or *that* it is. [Plato Works]

Doxastic, formed from δόξα, *opinion*, is the last of the gnostic powers of the rational soul; and knows *that* a thing is, but is ignorant of the cause of it, or *why* it is. The knowledge of the διοτι, or *why* a thing is, being the province of dianoia. [Procl. Theol. Plato.] [Procl. Comm. Timæus.]

Entheastically. In a divinely-inspired manner. [Procl. Comm. Timæus.]

Epithymetic Part of the Soul, the, or that part of the soul which is the principle of all-various desires. But *desire* is well defined, by the Pythagoreans, to be a certain tendency, impulse, and appetite of the soul, in order to be filled with something, or to enjoy something present, or to be disposed according to some sensitive energy. They add, that there is also a desire of the contraries to these, and this is a desire of the evacuation and absence, and of having no sensible perception of certain things. [Procl. Comm. Timæus.]

Eternal, the, το αιωνιον, that which has a never-ending subsistence, without any connection with time; or, as Plotinus profoundly defines it, infinite life at once total and full. [Plato Works]

Generation, γενεσις. An essence composite and multiform, and conjoined with time. This is the proper signification of the word; but it is used symbolically by Plato, and also by theologists more ancient than Plato, for the sake of indication. For as Proclus beautifully observes (in MS. Comment. in Parmenidem.), "Fables call the ineffable unfolding into light through causes, generation." "Hence," he adds, "in the Orphic writings, the first cause is denominated time; for where there is generation, according to its proper signification, there also there is time." [Plato Works]

Generation. A flowing condition of being, or a subsistence in becoming to be. Hence, *to gignesthai* signifies an extension in subsistence, or a tendency to being. [Procl. Comm. Timæus.]

Generated, that which is, το γενητον. That which has not the whole of its essence or energy subsisting at once, without temporal dispersion. [Plato Works]

Genesiurgic, the. That which is effective of generation. [Procl. Comm. Timæus.]

Guest, ξενος. This word, in its more ample signification in the Greek, denotes a *stranger*, but properly implies one who receives another, or is himself received at an entertainment. In [the Platonic] dialogues, therefore, wherever one of the speakers is introduced as a ξενος, I have translated this word *guest*, as being more conformable to the genius of Plato's dialogues, which may be justly called rich mental banquets, and consequently the speakers in them may be considered as so many guests. Hence in the Timæus, the persons of that dialogue are expressly spoken of as guests. [Plato Works] [Procl. Theol. Plato.]

Hyparxis, υπαρξις. The first principle or foundation, as it were, of the essence of a thing. Hence, also, it is the summit of essence. [Plato Works] [Procl. Comm. Timæus.] [Procl. Theol. Plato.]

Iconically. A thing is said to subsist *iconically,* when it subsists after the manner of an image. [Procl. Comm. Timæus.]

Idiom, ιδιωμα. The characteristic peculiarity of a thing. [Plato Works]

Idolically. Adumbratively. [Procl. Comm. Timæus.]

Immortal, the,[2] το αθανατον. According to Plato, there are many orders of immortality, pervading from on high to the last of things; and the ultimate echo, as it were, of immortality, is seen in the perpetuity of the mundane wholes, which according to the doctrine of the Elean Guest in the Politicus, they participate from the Father of the universe. For both the being and the life of every body depend on another cause; since body is not itself naturally adapted to connect, or adorn, or preserve itself. But the immortality of partial souls, such as ours, is more manifest and more perfect than this of the perpetual bodies in the universe; as is evident from the many demonstrations which are given of it in the Phædo, and in the 10th book of the Republic. For the immortality of partial souls has a more principal subsistence, as possessing in itself the cause of eternal permanency. But prior to both these is the immortality of dæmons; for these neither verge to mortality, nor are filled with the nature of things which are generated and corrupted. More venerable, however, than these, and essentially transcending them, is the immortality of divine souls, which are primarily self-motive, and contain the fountains and principles of the life which is attributed about bodies, and through which bodies participate of renewed immortality. And prior to all these is the immortality of the gods; for Diotima in the Banquet does not ascribe an immortality of this kind to dæmons. Hence such an immortality as this is separate and exempt from wholes. For, together with the immortality of the gods, eternity subsists, which is the fountain of all immortality and life, as well as that life which is perpetual, as that which is dissipated into nonentity. In short, therefore, the *divine immortal* is that which is generative and connective of perpetual life. For it is not immortal, as participating of life, but as supplying divine life, and deifying life itself. [Plato Works]

Imparticipable, το αμεθεκτον. That which is not consubsistent with an inferior nature. Thus imparticipable intellect is an intellect which is not consubsistent with soul. [Plato Works]
Imparticipable, αμεθεκτος. One thing is said to be imparticipable with respect to another, to which it is superior, when it is not consubsistent with it. [Procl. Theol. Plato.]

Intellect (*nous*), in the human soul is the summit of *dianoia*, and is that power by the light proceeding from which, we perceive the truth of axioms. But in divine natures it is a self-subsistent, impartible, eternal essence, perceiving all things at once. [Procl. Comm. Timæus.]

Intellectual Projection, νοερα επιβολη. As the perception of intellect is immediate, being a darting forth, as it were, directly to its proper objects, this direct intuition is expressed by the term *projection*. [Plato Works]

Intellectual projection. The immediate energy of intellect is thus denominated, because it is an intuitive perception, or an immediate darting forth, as it were, to its proper object, the intelligible. [Procl. Theol. Plato.] [Procl. Comm. Timæus.]

Intelligible, the, το νοητον. This word in Plato and Platonic writers has a various signification: for, in the first place, whatever is exempt from sensibles, and has its essence separate from them, is said to be intelligible, and in this sense soul is intelligible. In the second place, intellect, which is prior to soul, is intelligible. In the third place, that which is more ancient than intellect, which replenishes intelligence, and is essentially perfective of it, is called *intelligible:* and this is the intelligible, which Timæus in Plato places in the order of a paradigm, prior to the demiurgic intellect and intellectual energy. But beyond these is the *divine* intelligible, which is defined according to divine union and hyparxis. For this is intelligible as the object of desire to intellect, as giving perfection to and containing it, and as the completion of being. The highest intelligible, therefore, is that which is the hyparxis of the gods; the second, that which is true being, and the first essence; the third, intellect, and all intellectual life; and the fourth, the order belonging to soul. [Plato Works]

Intelligible, or Intellectual, or Psychical Breadth; *i.e.* the extent of the progression of the intelligible, of intellect and of soul, and of each of these according to its own order, and not according to a progression into an inferior order. [Procl. Comm. Timæus.]

Logismos, *reasoning.* When applied to divinity as by Plato, in the Timæus, signifies a distributive cause of things. [Plato Works]

Logos (see Reason)

Monad, μονας, in divine natures is that which contains *distinct*, but at the same time *profoundly-united* multitude, and which produces a multitude exquisitely allied to itself. But in the sensible universe, the first monad is the world itself, which comprehends in itself all the multitude of which it is the cause (in conjunction with the cause of all). The second monad is the inerratic sphere. In the third place, the spheres of the planets succeed, each of which is also a monad, comprehending an appropriate multitude. And in the fourth and last place are the spheres of the elements, which are in a similar manner monads. All these monads likewise are denominated ολοτητες, *wholenesses*, and have a perpetual subsistence. [Procl. Theol. Plato.]

Morphe. Pertains to the colour, figure, and magnitude of superficies. [Procl. Comm. Timæus.]

Multipotent. Possessing much power. [Procl. Comm. Timæus.]

On account of which; with reference to which; through which; according to which; from which; or in which; *viz.* δι ο, προς ο, υφ' ου, δι ου, καθ' ο, εξ ου. By the first of these terms, Plato is accustomed to denominate the final cause; by the second the paradigmatic; by the third the demiurgic; by the fourth the instrumental; by the fifth form; and by the sixth matter. [Plato Works]

Opinion (see Doxastic)

Orectic. This word is derived from *orexis,* appetite. [Plato Works]

Paradigm, παραδειγμα. A pattern, or that with reference to which a thing is made. [Plato Works]

Permanency, στασις. The proper word for rest, in Greek, is ηρεμια. And Simplicius justly observes, that not every στασις is ηρεμια, but that only which is after motion. This word is employed by Plato in the Sophista, to express one of the five genera of being, *viz. essence, permanency* (στασις)*, motion, sameness, and difference;* in which place it evidently does not signify rest. [Procl. Theol. Plato.]

Perpetual, the, το αιδιον. That which subsists forever, but through a connection with time. [Plato Works]

Phantasy, or *Imagination*, φαντασια, is, μορφωτικη νοησις, *i.e. a figured intelligence*, because all the perceptions of this power are *inward*, and not external, like those of sense, and are accompanied with *figure*. [Procl. Theol. Plato.]

Philopolemic. An epithet of Minerva, signifying that she is *a lover of war;* just as she is also called *philosophic,* as being *a lover of wisdom.* [Procl. Comm. Timæus.]

Plenitude (*pleroma*), or **Completeness.** Is a whole which gives completion to the universe. [Procl. Comm. Timæus.]

Politician, πολιτικος. This word, as Mr. Sydenham justly observes in his notes on the Rivals, is of a very large and extensive import, as used by Plato, and the other ancient writers on politics: for it includes all those statesmen or politicians in aristocracies and democracies who were, either for life, or for a certain time, invested with the whole or a part of kingly authority, and the power thereto belonging. See the Politicus. [Plato Works]

Prudence, φρονησις. This word frequently means in Plato and Platonic writers, the habit of discerning what is good in all moral actions, and frequently signifies intelligence, or intellectual perception. The following admirable explanation of this word is given by Iamblichus.

"Prudence having a precedaneous subsistence, receives its generation from a pure and perfect intellect. Hence it looks to intellect itself, is perfected by it, and has this as the measure and most beautiful paradigm of all its energies. If also we have any communion with the gods, it is especially effected by this virtue; and through this we are in the highest degree assimilated to them. The knowledge too of such things as are good, profitable, and beautiful, and of the contraries to these, is obtained by this virtue; and the judgment and correction of works proper to be done are by this directed. And in short it is a certain governing leader of men, and of the whole arrangement of their nature;

and referring cities and houses, and the particular life of every one, to a divine paradigm, it forms them according to the best similitude; obliterating some things and purifying others. So that prudence renders its possessors similar to divinity." Iamblic. apud. Stob. p. 141. [Plato Works]

Psychical, ψυχικος. Pertaining to soul. [Plato Works]

Psychical, ψυχικος, i.e. *pertaining to soul,* in the same manner as φυσικος, *physical,* is *something pertaining to nature.* [Procl. Theol. Plato.]

Reason, λογος. This word in Platonic writers signifies either that inward discursive energy called reasoning; or a certain productive and seminal principle; or that which is indicative and definitive of a thing. Hence λογοι or reasons in the soul, are, gnostically producing principles. [Procl. Theol. Plato.]

Reasons. *(logoi)* Productive principles or powers; and they also signify forms. [Procl. Comm. Timæus.]

Science. This word is sometimes defined by Plato to be that which assigns the causes of things; sometimes to be that the subjects of which have a perfectly stable essence; and together with this, he conjoins the assignation of cause from reasoning. Sometimes again he defines it to be that the principles of which are not hypotheses; and, according to this definition, he asserts that there is one science which ascends as far as to the principle of things. For this science considers that which is truly the principle as unhypothetic, has for its subject true being, and produces its reasonings from cause. According to the second definition, he calls dianoëtic knowledge science; but according to the first alone, he assigns to physiology the appellation of science. [Plato Works]

Telestic Art, the. The art pertaining to mystic operations. [Plato Works] [Procl. Comm. Timæus.]

Theurgic. This word is derived from θεουργια, or that religious operation which deifies him by whom it is performed as much as is possible to man. [Plato Works]

Truth, αληθεια. Plato, following ancient theologists, considers truth multifariously. Hence, according to his doctrine, the highest truth is characterized by unity; and is the light proceeding from *the good*, which imparts *purity*, as he says in the Philebus, and *union*, as he says in the Republic, to intelligibles. The truth which is next to this in dignity is that which proceeds from intelligibles, and illuminates the intellectual orders, and which an essence unfigured, uncoloured, and without contact, first receives, where also the plain of truth is situated, as it is written in the Phædrus. The third kind of truth is that which is connascent with souls, and which through intelligence comes into contact with true being. For the psychical light is the third from the intelligible; intellectual deriving its plenitude from intelligible light, and the psychical from the intellectual. And the last kind of truth is that which is in sensibles, which is full of error and inaccuracy through sense, and the instability of its object. For a material nature is perpetually flowing, and is not naturally adapted to abide even for a moment. The following beautiful description of the third kind of truth, or that which subsists in souls, is given by Iamblichus:

> "Truth, as the name implies, makes a conversion about the gods and their incorporeal energy; but doxastic imitation, which, as Plato says, is fabricative of images, wanders about that which is deprived of divinity and is dark. And the former indeed receives its perfection in intelligible and divine forms, and real beings which have a perpetual sameness of subsistence; but the latter looks to that which is formless, and non-being, and which has a various subsistence; and about this its visive power is blunted. The former contemplates that which is; but the latter assumes such a form as appears to the many. Hence the former associates with intellect, and increases the intellectual nature which we contain; but the latter, from looking to that which always seems to be, hunts after folly and deceives." Iamblic. apud. Stob. p. 136. [Plato Works]

Unical, ενιαιος, that which is characterized by unity. [Plato Works] [Procl. Theol. Plato.]

Unically. In a way conformable to the nature of *The One*. [Procl. Comm. Timæus.]

Uniform, ενοειδης. This word when it occurs in Proclus, and other Platonic writers, signifies that which has the form of *the one*, and not as in Johnson, that which keeps its tenour, or is similar to itself. [Procl. Theol. Plato.]

Wholeness. A whole which has a perpetual subsistence, and which comprehends in itself all the multitude of which it is the cause. [Procl. Comm. Timæus.]

The

Life of Plato

by Olympiodorus

Let us now speak of the race of the philosopher, not for the sake of relating many particulars concerning him, but rather with a view to the advantage and instruction of his readers; since he was by no means an obscure man, but one who attracted the attention of many. For it is said that the father of Plato was Aristo, the son of Aristocles, from who he refers his origin to Solon the legislator. Hence with primitive zeal he wrote twelve books of Laws, and eleven books on a Republic. But his mother was Perictione, who descended from Neleus the son of Codrus.

They say then that an Apolloniacal spectre[1] had connection with his mother Perictione, and that, appearing in the night to Aristo, it commanded him not to sleep with Perictione during the time of her pregnancy—which mandate Aristo obeyed.

While he was yet an infant, his parents are said to have placed him in Hymettus, being desirous, on his account, to sacrifice to the Gods of that mountain, *viz.* Pan, and the Nymphs, and the pastoral Apollo. In the mean time the bees, approaching as he lay, filled his mouth with honeycombs, as an omen that in future it might truly be said of him,

Words from his tongue than honey sweeter flowed.[2]

But Plato calls himself a fellow-servant with swans, as deriving his origin from Apollo; for according to the Greeks that bird is Apolloniacal.

When he was a young man, he first betook himself to Dionysius the grammarian for the purpose of acquiring common literature. Of this Dionysius he makes mention in his dialogue called The Lovers— that even Dionysius the school-master might not be passed over in silence by Plato. After him he employed the argive Aristo, as his instructor in gymnastic,[3] from whom he is said to have derived the name of Plato; for prior to this he was called Aristocles, from his grandfather: but he was so called from having those parts of the body the breast and forehead broad in the extreme, as his statues every where evince. According to others, however, he was called Plato from the ample and expanded character of his style; just as they say Theophrastus was so called, from his divine eloquence, his first name being Tyrtamus.

For his preceptor in music Plato had Draco, the son of Damon; and of this master he makes mention in his Republic. For the Athenians instructed their children in these three arts, *viz.* grammar, music, and gymnastic—and this, as it seems, with great propriety. They taught them grammar, for the purpose of adorning their reason; music, that they might tame their anger; and gymnastic, that they might strengthen the weak tone of desire. Alcibiades also, in Plato, appears to have been instructed in these three disciplines; and hence Socrates says to him, "But you were unwilling to play on the pipe," etc. He was also conversant with painters, from whom he learned the mixture of colours, of which he makes mention in the Timæus.

After this he was instructed by the Tragedians, who at that time were celebrated as the preceptors of Greece: but he betook himself to these writers on account of the sententious and venerable nature of tragic composition, and the heroic sublimity of the subjects. He was likewise conversant with Dithyrambic writers, with a view to the honour of Bacchus, who was called by the Greeks the inspective guardian of generation: for the Dithyrambic measure is sacred to Bacchus, from whom also it derives its name; Bacchus being Dithyrambus, as proceeding into light from two avenues—the womb of Semele, and the thigh of Jupiter. For the ancients were accustomed to call effects by the names of their causes, as in the name Dithyrambus given to Bacchus. Hence Proclus observes:

With their late offspring parents seem to mix.

But that Plato applied himself to Dithyrambics is evident from his Phædrus, which plainly breathes the Dithyrambic character, and is said to have been the first dialogue which Plato composed.

He was also much delighted with the comic Aristophanes and Sophron,[4] from whom he learned the imitations of persons in dialogues. He is said to have been so much pleased with the writings of these men, that, on his death, they were found in his bed. Plato himself likewise composed the following epigram on Aristophanes:

The Graces, once intent to find
A temple which might ne'er decay,
The soul of Aristophanes
At length discover'd in their way.

He reproves him, however, in a comic manner in his dialogue called The Banquet, in which he gives a specimen of his proficiency in comedy: for here Plato introduces him celebrating Love, and in the midst of his oration seized with a hiccup, so as to be unable to finish it. Plato also composed Tragic and Dithyrambic poems, and some other poetical pieces, all which he burned as soon as he began to associate with Socrates, at the same time repeating this verse:

Vulcan! draw near; 'tis Plato asks your aid.[5]

Anatolius the grammarian, once reciting this verse, very much pleased Vulcan, at that time the governor of the city. But he thus addressed him:

Vulcan! draw near; 'tis Pharos[6] asks your aid.

It is said, that when Socrates first intended to receive Plato as his disciple, he saw in a dream a swan without wings sitting on his bosom, which soon after obtaining wings flew into the air, and with the sweetness of its shrill voice allured all those that heard it. This was a manifest token of Plato's future renown.

After the death of Socrates he had another preceptor, the Heraclitean Cratylus, upon whom he also composed a dialogue, which is inscribed Cratylus, or, Concerning the rectitude of names. After he had been sufficiently instructed by this master, he again went into Italy, where finding Archytas restoring a Pythagoric school, he again had a Pythagoric preceptor of this name; and hence it is that he makes mention of Archytas. But since it is requisite that a philosopher should desire to behold the works of nature, he also went into Sicily for the purpose of viewing the eruptions of fire in Mount Ætna, and not for the sake of the Sicilian table, as you, O noble Aristides, assert.

When he was in Syracuse with Dionysius the Great, who was a tyrant, he endeavoured to change the tyranny into an aristocracy; and it was for this purpose that he visited the tyrant. But Dionysius asking him whom among men he considered as happy? (for he thought that the philosopher, employing flattery, would speak of him,) Plato answered, "Socrates." Again the tyrant asked him, "What do you think is the business of a politician?" Plato answered, "To make the citizens better." He again asked him the third time, "What, then, does it appear to you to be a small matter to decide rightly in judicial affairs?" (for Dionysius was celebrated for deciding in such affairs with rectitude.) Plato answered boldly, "It is a small matter, and the last part of good conduct; for those who judge rightly resemble such as repair lacerated garments." Again Dionysius asked him the fourth time, "Must not he who is a tyrant be brave?" Plato replied, "He is of all men the most timid; for he even dreads the razors of his barbers, lest he should be destroyed by them." With these answers Dionysius was so indignant, that he ordered him to depart at sunrise.

The following was the cause of his second journey to Sicily. When, after the death of Dionysius the tyrant, his son succeeded to the throne, who by his mother's side was the brother of Dion, with whom Plato became acquainted in his first journey, Plato again sailed to Sicily, at the solicitations of Dion, who told him it might now be hoped that through his exertions the tyranny might be changed into an aristocracy. However, as Dionysius had been told by some of his attendants that Plato designed to destroy him, and transfer the government to Dion, he ordered him to be taken into custody, and delivered to one Pollidis of Ægina, a Sicilian merchant, to be sold as a slave. But Pollidis taking Plato to Ægina found there the Libyan Anniceris, who was then on the point of sailing to Elis, for the purpose of contending with the four-yoked car. Anniceris gladly bought Plato of Pollidis, conceiving that he should thence procure for himself greater glory than by conquering in the race. Hence Aristides observes, that no one would have known Anniceris, if he had not bought Plato.

The following circumstance was the occasion of Plato's third journey to Sicily. Dion, being proscribed by Dionysius, and deprived of his possessions, was at length cast into prison. He therefore wrote to Plato, that Dionysius had promised to liberate him, if Plato would again visit him. But Plato, that he might afford assistance to his associate, readily undertook this third voyage. And thus much for the journeys of the philosopher into Sicily.

Plato likewise went into Egypt for the purpose of conversing with the priests of that country, and from them learned whatever pertains to sacred rites. Hence in his Gorgias he says, "Not by the dog, who is considered as a God by the Egyptians." For animals among the Egyptians effect the same things as statues among the Greeks, as being symbols of the several deities to which they are dedicated. However, as he wished to converse with the Magi, but was prevented by the war which at that time broke out in Persia, he went to Phœnicia, and, meeting with the Magi of that country, he was instructed by them in magic. Hence, from his Timæus, he appears to have been skilful in divination; for he there speaks of the signs of the liver, of the viscera, and the like. These things, however, ought to have been mentioned prior to his journeys to Sicily.

When he return to Athens he established a school in the Academy, separating a part of this Gymnasium into a temple to the Muses. Here Timon the misanthrope associated with Plato alone. But Plato allured very many to philosophical discipline, preparing men and also women[7] in a virile habit to be his auditors, and evincing that his philosophy deserved the greatest voluntary labour: for he avoided the Socratic irony, nor did he converse in the Forum and in workshops, nor endeavour to captivate young men by his discourses. Add too, that he did not adopt the venerable oath of the Pythagoreans, their custom of keeping their gates shut, and their *ipse dixit*, as he wished to conduct himself in a more political manner towards all men.

When he was near his death, he appeared to himself in a dream to be changed into a swan, who, by passing from tree to tree, caused much labour to the fowlers. According to the Socratic Simmias, this dream signified that his meaning would be apprehended with difficulty by those who should be desirous to unfold it after his death. For interpreters resemble fowlers, in their endeavours to explain the conceptions of the ancients. But his meaning cannot be apprehended without great difficulty, because his writings, like those of Homer, are to be considered physically, ethically, theologically, and, in short, multifariously; for those two souls are said to have been generated all-harmonic: and hence the writings of both Homer and Plato demand an all-various consideration. Plato was sumptuously buried[8] by the Athenians; and on his sepulchre they inscribed the following epitaph:

> From great Apollo Pæon sprung,
>   And Plato too we find;
> The saviour of the body one,
>   The other of the mind.

And thus much concerning the race of the philosopher.

Notes

General Introduction

1. Φιλοσοφια εστι ζωης ανθρηπινης καθαρσις, και τελειοτης· καθαρσις μεν, απο της υλικης αλογιας, και του θνητοειδους σωματος· τελειοτης δε, της οικειας ευξωιας αναληψις, προς την θειαν ομοιωσιν επαναγουσα. Ταυτα δε πεφυκεν αρετη και αληθεια μαλιστα απεργαξεσθαι· η μεν την αμετριαν των παθων εξοριζουσα· η δε το θειον ειδος τοις ευφνως εχουσι προσκτωμενη. Hierocl. in Aur. Carm. p. 9. edit. Needh.

2. In the mysteries a light of this kind shone forth from the adytum of the temple in which they were exhibited.

3. Odyss. V. v. 281.

4. This most excellent philosopher, whose MS. treatise περι αρχων is a treasury of divine science and erudition, is justly called by Simplicius ζητικωτατος, most inquisitive. See a very long and beautiful extract from this work in the Additional Notes on the third volume.

5. See the Sophista of Plato, where this is asserted.

6. For a thing cannot be said to be a principle or cause without the subsistence of the things of which it is the principle or cause. Hence, so far as it is a principle or cause, it will be indigent of the subsistence of these.

7. See the extracts from Damascius in the additional notes to the third volume of the *Works of Plato*, which contain an inestimable treasury of the most profound conceptions concerning the ineffable.

8. Page 9, of the quarto edition.

9. By the first principle here, *the one* is to be understood: for that arcane nature which is beyond *the one*, since all language is subverted about it, can only, as we have already observed, be conceived and venerated in the most profound silence.

10. Τι δει πολλα λεγειν, οτε και τους θεους ουτως υποτιθεται τους πολλους, οι προ Ιαμβλιχου σχεδον παντες φιλοσοφοι ενα μεν ειναι τον υπερουσιον θεον λεγοντες, τους αλλους ουσιωδεις ειναι, ταις απο του ενος ελλαμψεσιν εκθεουμενους, και ειναι το των υπερουσιων πληθος εναδων, ουκ αυτοτελων υποστασεων, αλλα των ελλαμπομενων απο του μονου θεου, και ταις ουσιαις ενδιδομενων θεωσεων. Damasc. Περι Αρχων. MS.

11. See vol. III., p. 133, *Works of Plato*, 1804.

12. As we have shown in the note to p. 133, vol. III., *Works of Plato*.

13. See vol. III., p. 500, *Works of Plato*, 1804. See also a copious account of the nature of dæmons in additional notes to the First Alcibiades, vol. I.

14. Αγε δη ουν, ειπερ ποτε, και νυν τας πολυειδις; αποσκευασωμεθα γνωσεις, και παν το ποικιλον της ζωης εξωρισωμεν αφ' ημων, και παντων εν ηρεμια γενομενος,

τω παντων αιτιω προσιωμεν εγγυς. Εστω δε ημιν μη μονον δοξης, μηδε φαντασιας ηρεμια, μηδε ησυχια των παθων ημων εμποδιζοντων την προς το πρωτον αναγωγον ορμην αλλ' ησυχος μεν αηρ, ησυχον δε το παν τουτο· παντα δε ατρεμει τη δυναμει προς την του αρρητου μετουσιαν ημας ανατεινετω. Και σταντεσ εκαι, και το νοητον (ει δη τι τοιουτον εστιν εν ημιν) υπερδραμοντες, και οιον ηλιον ανισχοντα προσκυνησαντες, μεμυκοσι τοις οφθαλμοις (ου γαρ θεμις αντωπειν ουδε αλλο των οντων ουδεν) τον τοινυν του φωτος των νοητων θεων ηλιον εξ ωκεανου, φασιν οι ποιηται, προφαινομειον ιδοντες, και αυθις εκ της ενθεου ταυτης γαληνης εις νουν καταβαντες, και απο νου τοις της ψυχης χρωμενοι λογισμοις, ειπωμεν προς ημας αυτους, ων εξηρημενον εν τη πορεια ταυτη τον πρωτον θεον τεθειμεθα. Και οιον υμνησωμεν αυτον ουχ οτι γην, και ουρανον υπεστησεν λεγοντες, ουδ αυ οτι ψυχας, και ζωων απαντων γενεσεις, και ταυτα μεν γαρ, αλλ' επ' εσχατοις· προ δε τουτων, ως παν μεν το νοητον των θεων γενος, παν δε το νοερον εξεφηνε, πα τας δε τους υπερ τον κοσμον, και τους εν τω κοσμω θεους απαντας, και ως θεος εστι θεων απαντων, και ως ειας εναδων, και ως των αδυνατων (lege αδυτων) επεκεινα των πρωτων, και ως πασης σιγης αρρητοτερον, και ως πασης υπαρξεως αγνωστοτερον, αγοις εν αγιοις, τοις νοητοις εναποκεκρυμμενοσ θεοις. Proc. In Plat. Theol. p. 109.

15. Lib. xix. v. 40.

16. Vol. iii, *Works of Plato*, near the end. See also the notes on the seventh epistle of Plato.

17. It is necessary to observe, that, according to Plato, whatever participates of any thing is said to be *passive* to that which it participates, and the participations themselves are called by him *passions*.

18. In Plat. Theol. lib. i, cap. 4.

19. The following excellent account of the different species of fables is given by the philosopher Sallust, in his book *On the Gods and the World*, chap iv:

"Of fables, some are theological, others physical, others animastic, (or belonging to soul,) others material, and lastly, others mixed from these. Fables are theological which employ nothing corporeal, but speculate the very essences of the gods; such as the fable which asserts that Saturn devoured his children: for it obscurely intimates the nature of an intellectual god, since every intellect returns into itself. But we speculate fables physically when we speak concerning the energies of the gods about the world; as when considering Saturn the same as Time, and calling the parts of time the children of the universe, we assert that the children are devoured by their parents. But we employ fables in an animastic mode when we contemplate the energies of soul; because the intellections of our souls, though by a discursive energy they proceed into other things, yet abide in their parents. Lastly, fables are material, such as the Egyptians ignorantly employ, considering and calling corporeal natures divinities; such as Isis, earth; Osiris, humidity;

Typhon, heat: or again, denominating Saturn, water; Adonis, fruits; and Bacchus, wine. And, indeed, to assert that these are dedicated to the gods, in the same manner as herbs, stones, and animals, is the part of wise men; but to call them gods is alone the province of mad men; unless we speak in the same manner as when, from established custom, we call the orb of the Sun and its rays the Sun itself.

"But we may perceive the mixed kind of fables, as well in many other particulars, as in the fable which relates, that Discord at a banquet of the gods threw a golden apple, and that a dispute about it arising among the goddesses, they were sent by Jupiter to take the judgement of Paris, who, charmed with the beauty of Venus, gave her the apple in preference to the rest. For in this fable the banquet denotes the supermundane powers of the gods; and on this account they subsist in conjunction with each other: but the golden apple denotes the world, which, on account of its composition from contrary natures, is not improperly said to be thrown by Discord, or strife. But again, since different gifts are imparted to the world by different gods, they appear to contest with each other for the apple. And a soul living according to sense, (for this is Paris) not perceiving other powers in the universe, asserts that the contended apple subsists alone through the beauty of Venus. But of these species of fables, such as are theological belong to philosophers; the physical and animastic to poets; but the mixed to initiatory rites since the intention of all mystic ceremonies is, to conjoin us with the world and the gods."

See more concerning this last species of fables in my "Dissertation on the Eleusinian and Bacchic Mysteries."

20. In Plat. Theol. lib i, cap. 5, etc.

21. A whole prior to parts is that which causally contains parts in itself. Such parts too, when they proceed from their occult causal subsistence, and have a distinct being of their own, are nevertheless comprehended, though in a different manner, in their producing whole.

22. The principle of all things is celebrated by Platonic philosophy as the cause of wholes, because through transcendency of power he first produces those powers in the universe which rank as wholes, and afterwards those which rank as parts, through these. Agreeably to this Jupiter, the artificer of the universe, is almost always called δεμιουργος των ολων, the *demiurgus* of wholes. See the Timæus, and the Introduction to it.

23. See my translation of Aristotle's Metaphysics, p. 347. If the reader conjoins what is said concerning ideas in the notes on that work, with the introduction and notes to the Parmenides, he will be in possession of nearly all that is to be found in the writings of the ancients on this subject.

24. It appears from this passage of Syrianus that Longinus was the original inventor of the theory of abstract ideas; and that Mr. Locke was merely the restorer of it.

25. This was a Greek philosopher, who is often cited by Simplicius in his Commentary on the Predicaments, and must not therefore be confounded with Boetius, the Roman senator and philosopher.

26. For an account of this order, see the Introduction to the Timæus, and the notes on the Parmenides.

27. In the Phædo Plato discourses on the former of these virtues, and in the Theætetus on the latter.

28. υγιης τε και ολοκληρος γενομενος εις το της προτερας αφικοιτο ειδος εξεως.

29. Διο δει ενθενδε εκεισε φυγειν· φυγη δε ομοιωσις θεω κατα το δυνατον ανθρωπω· ομοιωσις δε, δικαιον και οσιον μετα φρονησεως γενεσθαι.

30. Ο μεγας αγων, και ελπις η μεγαλη.

31. See the Additional Notes on the First Alcibiades, *Works of Plato*, p. 500.

32. Vid. Alcin. de Doctr. Plat. cap. v.

33. See the ancient Latin version of Proclus on Providence and Fate, in the 8th volume of the Biblioth. Græc. of Fabricius.

34. A line of Epicharmus. See the Phædo.

35. See the Second Analytics of Aristotle.

36. That this must be the tendency of experiment, when prosecuted as the criterion of truth, is evident from what Bacon, the prince of modern philosophy, says in the 104th Aphorism of his Novum Organum, that *"baseless fabric of a vision."* For he there *sagely* observes that wings are not to be added to the human intellect, but rather lead and weights; that all its leaps and flights may be restrained. That this is not yet done, but that when it is we may entertain better hopes respecting the sciences.

> "Itaque hominum intellectui non plumæ addendæ, sed plumbum potius, et pondera; ut cohibeant omnem saltum et volatum. Atque hoc adhuc factum non est; quum vero factum fuerit, melius de scientiis sperare licebit."

A considerable portion of lead must certainly have been added to the intellect of Bacon when he wrote this Aphorism.

37. I never yet knew a man who made experiment the test of truth, and I have known many such, that was not atheistically inclined.

38. I have ranked Archimedes among the Platonists, because he cultivated the mathematical sciences Platonically, as is evident from the testimony of Plutarch in his Life of Marcellus, p.307. For he there informs us that Archimedes considered the being busied about mechanics, and in short every art which is connected with the common purposes of life, as ignoble and illiberal; and that those things alone were objects of his ambition with which

the beautiful and the excellent were present, unmingled with the necessary,—
αλλα την περι τα μηχανικα πραγματειαν, και πασαν ολως τεχνην χρειας
εφαπτομενην, αγεννη και βαναυσον ηγησαμενος, εκεινα καταθεσθαι μονα την
αυτου φιλοτιμιαν, οις το καλον και περιττον αμιγες του αναγκαιου προσεστιν.—
The great accuracy and elegance in the demonstrations of Euclid and
Archimedes, which have not been equalled by any of our greatest modern
mathematicians, were derived from a deep conviction of this important truth.
On the other hand modern mathematicians, through a profound ignorance of
this divine truth, and looking to nothing but the wants and conveniences of
the animal life of man, as if the gratification of his senses was his only end,
have corrupted pure geometry, by mingling with it algebraical calculations,
and through eagerness to reduce it as much as possible to practical purposes,
have more anxiously sought after conciseness than accuracy, facility than
elegance of geometrical demonstration.

39. Επι των λεγομενων τελετων, τα μεν αδυτα ην, ως δηλοι και τουνοαα τα δε
παραπετασματα, προβεβληνται, αθεατα τα εν τοις αδυτοις φυλαττονται. Psellus
in Alleg. de Sphin.

40. See my Dissertation on the Mysteries.

41. See the 7th Epistle of Plato.

42. It would seem that those intemperate critics who have thought proper to
revile Plotinus, the leader of the latter Platonists, have paid no attention to the
testimony of Longinus concerning this most wonderful man, as preserved by
Porphyry in his life of him. For Longinus there says, that

> "though he does not entirely accede to many of his hypotheses, yet he
> exceedingly admires and loves the form of his writing, the density of
> his conceptions, and the philosophic manner in which his questions are
> disposed."*

And in another place he says:

> "Plotinus, as it seems, has explained the Pythagoric and Platonic
> principles more clearly than those that were prior to him; for neither
> are the writings of Numenius, Cronius, Moderatus, and Thrasyllus, to
> be compared for accuracy with those of Plotinus on this subject."†

After such a testimony as this from such a consummate critic as Longinus, the
writings of Plotinus have nothing to fear from the imbecile censure of
modern critics. I shall only further observe, that Longinus, in the above
testimony, does not give the least hint of his having found any *polluted
streams*, or corruption of the doctrines of Plato, in the works of Plotinus.
There is not indeed the least vestige of his entertaining any such opinion in
any part of what he has said about this most extraordinary man. This discovery
was reserved for the more acute critic of modern times, who, by a happiness of

conjecture unknown to the ancients, and the assistance of a good index, can in a few days penetrate the meaning of the profoundest writer of antiquity, and bid defiance even to the decision of Longinus.

---

* Οτι των μεν υποθεσεων ου πανυ με τας πολλας προσιεσθαι συμβεβηκεν, τον δε τυπον της γραφης και των εννοιων τ' ανδρος την πυκνοτητα, και το φιλοσοφον της των ζητηματων διαθεσεως υπερβαλλοντως αγαμαι και φιλω.

† Ος μεν τας Πυθαγορειους αρχας και Πλατωνικας, ως εδοκει, προς σαφεστεραν προ αυτου καταστησαμενος εξηγησεν· ουδε γαρ ουδ' ηγγυς τι τα Νουμηνιου, και Κρονιου, και Μοδερατου και Θρασυλλου τοις Πλωτινου περι των αυτων συγγραμμασιν εις ακριβειαν.

43. Of this most divine man, who is justly said by the emperor Julian to have been posterior indeed in time, but not in genius even to Plato himself, see the life given in the History of the Restoration of the Platonic Theology, in the second vol. of my Proclus on Euclid.

44. Βιβλιοθηκην τινα εμψυχον και περιπατουν μουσειον.

45. Ο δε Πορφυριος ωσπερ Ερμαϊκη τις σειρα και προς ανθρωπους επινευουσα, δια ποικιλης παιδειας παντα εις το ευγνωστον και καθαρον εξηγγελεν.

46. Πασαν μεν αυτος ανατρεχων χαριν, μονος δε αναδεικνυς και ανακηρυττων τον διδασκαλον. Eunap. In Porphy. vit.

47. Επει δε παλιν υς εγρυξε κατα τον μελωδον Αλκαιον, παλιν αναγκη επι τον Γραμματικον τουτον προκυψαι. Simplicius de Philopono, in Comment. ad Aristot. de Coelo. p. 35, 6.

48. Pope's Odyssey, book xxii, v. 47, etc.

49. Εαν μη τις κατ' ειδη διαιπεισθαι τα οντα, και μια ιδεα δυνατος η καθ' εν εκαστον περιλαμβανειν, ουποτ' εσται τεχνικος λογων περι, καθ' οσον δυνατον ανθρωπῳ. Whoever is unable to divide and distinguish things into their several sorts or species; and, on the other hand, referring every particular to its proper species, to comprehend them all in one general idea; will never understand any writings, of which those things are the subject, like a true critic, upon those high principles of art to which the human understanding reaches. Πλατ. Φαιδρ. We have thought proper, here, to paraphrase this passage, for the sake of giving to every part of so important a sentence its full force, agreeably to the tenor of Plato's doctrine; and in order to initiate our readers into a way of thinking, that probably many of them are as yet unacquainted with.

50. See Διογ. Λαερτ. Βιβ. γ΄.

51. It is necessary to observe, that Plato in the Parmenides calls all that part of his Dialectic, which proceeds through opposite arguments, γυμνασια και πλανη, an *exercise* and *wandering*.

52. We have, given us by Diogenes Laertius, another division of the characters, as he calls them, of Plato's writings, different from that exhibited

in the scheme above. This we have thought proper to subjoin, on account of its antiquity and general reception.

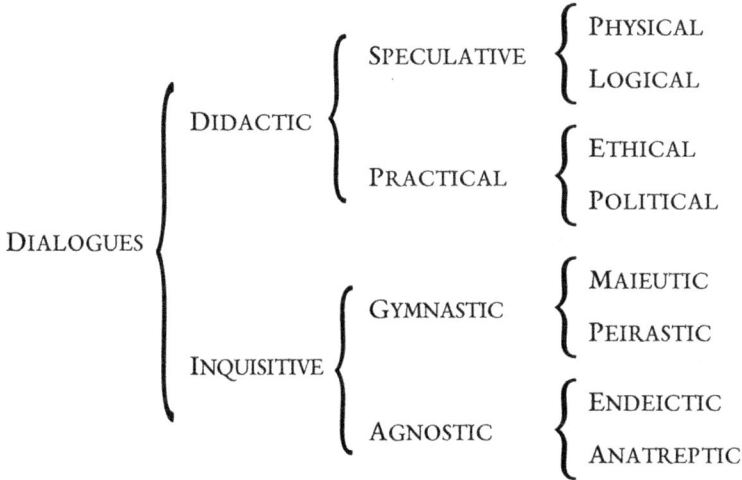

```
                                                          ┌ PHYSICAL
                                    ┌ SPECULATIVE ┤
                                    │                     └ LOGICAL
                       ┌ DIDACTIC ┤
                       │            │                     ┌ ETHICAL
                       │            └ PRACTICAL   ┤
                       │                                  └ POLITICAL
DIALOGUES ┤
                       │                                  ┌ MAIEUTIC
                       │            ┌ GYMNASTIC   ┤
                       │            │                     └ PEIRASTIC
                       └ INQUISITIVE ┤
                                    │                     ┌ ENDEICTIC
                                    └ AGNOSTIC    ┤
                                                          └ ANATREPTIC
```

The learned reader will observe the latter half of the dialogues, according to this scheme, to be described by metaphors taken from the gymnastic art: the dialogues, here termed gymnastic, being imagined to bear a similitude to that exercise; the agonistic, to the combat. In the lowest subdivision, indeed, the word *maieutic* is a metaphor of another kind, fully explained in Plato's Theætetus: the maieutic dialogues, however, were supposed to resemble giving the rudiments of the art; as the peirastic were, to represent a skirmish, or trial of proficiency: the endeictic were, it seems, likened to the exhibiting a specimen of skill; and the anatreptic, to presenting the spectacle of a thorough defeat, or sound drubbing.

The principal reason why we contented not ourselves with this account of the difference between the dialogues of Plato, was the capital error there committed in the first subdivision, of course extending itself through the latter. This error consists in dividing the Didactic dialogues with regard to their subject-matter; while those of the Inquisitive sort are divided with respect to the manner of their composition. So that the subdivisions fall not, with any propriety, under one and the same general head. Besides, a novice in the works of Plato might hence be led naturally to suppose, that the dogmatical or didactic dialogues are, all of them, written in the same manner; and that the others, those of the inquisitive kind, by us termed sceptical, have no particular subjects at all; or, if they have, that their subjects are different from those of the didactic dialogues, and are consequently unphilosophical. Now every one of the suppositions here mentioned is far from being true.

53. We require *exhortation*, that we may be led to true good; *dissuasion*, that

we may be turned from things truly evil; *obstetrication*, that we may draw forth our unperverted conceptions; and *confutation*, that we may be purified from two-fold ignorance.

54. The Platonists rightly observe, that Socrates, in these cases, makes use of demonstrative and just reasoning, (αποδεικτικου;) whereas to the novice he is contented with arguments only probable, (πιθανοις;) and against the litigious sophist often employs such as are (επιστικοι) puzzling and contentious. See Αλκιν. Εισαγωγ. Κεφ. στ΄.

55. It is necessary to observe, that in those dialogues, in which Socrates is indeed introduced, but sustains an inferior part, he is presented to our view as a *learner*, and not as a *teacher;* and this is the case in the Parmenides and Timæus. For by the former of these philosophers he is instructed in the most abstruse theological dogmas, and by the latter in the whole of physiology.

56. Επι γαρ τουτοις και τον Πλατονα ουχ ηκιστα διασυρουσι, πολλακις ωσπερ υπο βαμχειας τινος των λογων, εις ακρατους και απηνεις μεταφορας, και εις αλληγορικον στομφον εκφερομενον. Longin. Περι Υψους.

57. The reader will see, from the notes on Plato's dialogues, and particularly from the notes on the Parmenides and Timæus, that the style of that philosopher possesses an accuracy which is not to be found in any modern writer; an accuracy of such a wonderful nature, that the words are exactly commensurate with the sense. Hence the reader who has happily penetrated his profundity finds, with astonishment, that another word could not have been added without being superfluous, nor one word taken away without injuring the sense. The same observation may also be applied to the style of Aristotle.

58. As I profess to give the reader a translation of the genuine works of Plato only, I have not translated the Axiochus, Demodocus, Sisyphus, etc. as these are evidently spurious dialogues.

59. In the notes on the above-mentioned nine dialogues, those written by Mr. Sydenham are signed S., and those by myself T.

60. Patricius was one of the very few in modern times who have been sensible of the great merit of these writings, as is evident from his preface to his translation of Proclus's Theological Elements. (Ferrar. 4to. 1583.)

> "Extant in hoc Platonicæ Philosophiæ genere, etiam Hermiæ qui fuit Ammonii pater, commentaria elegantissima in Phædrum, nec non Olympiodori cujusdam longe doctissimi excerpta quædam ex ejus commentariis in Phædonem ac Philebum, et integra in Gorgiam. Sed omnium eminentissimæ, Damascii Questiones De Principiis rerum sunt. Quæ omnia si publice viserentur, ardentissimos divinæ sapientiæ amores excitarent, in iis pectoribus, quæ non argutandi causâ, sed modo hoc unum, ut sapiant, philosophiæ operam navant. Quæ si aliquando viri alicujus verè viri, opere quamvis laborioso, glorioso tamen in lucem

prodeant, apparebit tandem, quanta sapientiæ pars tenebris obruta jaceat, dum usitatam hanc in scholis solam sequimur, et amamus sapientiam. Cui rei manus dare, quantum vitæ et ocii suppetet, non deest nobis animus ingens. Utinam vita tranquillior, et fortuna adversa minus nobis contegisset, if jam forte totum confectum esset."

Patricius, prior to this, enumerates the writings of Proclus, and they are included in his wish, that all the manuscript Greek commentaries on Plato were made public.

61. I am pleased to find that this very respectable prelate is a great admirer of Aristotle, and that extracts from the Commentaries of Simplicius and Ammonius on the Categories of that philosopher, are read by his orders in the college of which he is the head.

62. Permit me also to mention, with gratitude for their kindness, the names of Dr. Stanley, Mr. Heber, the Rev. Mr. Coppleston, and the Rev. Abram Robertson, Savilian professor of geometry.

63. In Epist. ad Hipparchum.

Explanation of Certain Platonic Terms

1. See Procl. in Plat. Theol. p. 64.
2. See Procl. in Plat. Theol. p. 65.

Life of Plato by Olympiodorus

1. The like account of the divine origin of Plato is also given by Hesychius, Apuleius on the dogmas of Plato, and Plutarch in the eighth book of his Symposiacs. But however extraordinary this circumstance may appear, it is nothing more than one of those mythological relations in which heroes are said to have Gods for their fathers, or Goddesses for their mothers; and the true meaning of it is as follows:

According to the ancient theology, between those perpetual attendants of a divine nature called *essential* heroes, who are impassive and pure, and the bulk of human souls who descend to earth with passivity and impurity, it is necessary there should be an order of human souls who descend with impassivity and purity. For, as there is no vacuum either in incorporeal or corporeal natures, it is necessary that the last link of a superior order should coalesce with the summit of one proximately inferior. These souls were called by the ancients *terrestrial* heroes, on account of their high degree of proximity and alliance to such as are *essentially* heroes. Hercules, Theseus, Pythagoras, Plato, etc. were souls of this kind, who descended into mortality, both to benefit other souls, and in compliance with that necessity by which all natures inferior to the perpetual attendants of the Gods are at times obliged to descend.

But as, according to the arcana of ancient theology, every God beginning from on high produces his proper series as far as to the last of things, and this series comprehends many essences different from each other, such as Dæmonical, Heroical, Nymphical, and the like; the lowest powers of these orders have a great communion and physical sympathy with the human race, and contribute to the perfection of all their natural operations, and particularly to their procreations.

> "Hence," says Proclus in Cratylum, "it often appears that *heroes* are generated from the mixture of these powers with mankind; for those that possess a certain prerogative above human nature are properly denominated *heroes*."

He adds:

> "Not only a dæmoniacal genus of this kind sympathizes physically with men, but other kinds sympathize with other natures, as nymphs with trees, others with fountains, and others with stags or serpents."

See more on this interesting subject in the Notes to my translation of Pausanias, vol. iii, p. 229, etc.

Etwall, the editor of this Life, not being acquainted with the philosophical explanation of this MIRACULOUS CONCEPTION of Plato, pretends that this story originated from Plato being said to be born in the month Thargelion (with us, June), and on the very day in which Latona is reported to have brought forth Apollo and Diana.

2. Hom. Iliad lib. i ver. 249.

3. Some affirm that Plato so excelled in the gymnastic art, that he contended in the Pythian and Isthmian games. *Pythia et Isthmia de lucta certavit.* Apuleius de Dogmate Platonis.

4. This Sophron was a Syracusan, and contemporary with Euripides. He was an obscure writer; and his works, none of which are now extant, were in the Doric dialect.

5. According to the words of Homer, Iliad lib. xviii, ver. 392.

6. Pharos, as is well known, was a large tower near Alexandria, affording light to navigators in the night. Anatolius, therefore, in calling himself *Pharos* must have alluded to the etymology of his name. For *Anatolius* may be considered as being derived from ανατολη, the east, whence the light of the two great luminaries of heaven emerges, and φαρος may be said to be quasi φανος, because the light of torches appeared from it.

7. Two women particularly in a virile habit are said to have been his auditors, Lathsbenia the Mantinensian, and Axiothia the Phliasensian.

8. Plato was born six years after Isocrates, in the 87th Olympiad, and 430

years before Christ. He also died on his birthday, after having lived exactly 81 years. Hence, says Seneca, the MAGI, who then happened to be at Athens, sacrificed to him on his decease as a being more than human, because he had consummated a most perfect number, which 9 nine times multiplied produces.

Nam hoc seis puto, Platoni diligentiæ suæ beneficio contigisse, quod natali suo decessit, et annum unum atque octogesimum implevit, sine ullâ deductione. Ideo MAGI, qui fortè Athenis erant, immolaverunt defuncto, amplioris suisse fortis, quam humanæ, rait quia consummâsset perfectissimum numerum, quem novem novies multiplicata componunt. Senec. Epist. 63.

Printed in Great Britain
by Amazon

62397301R00070